Solve That Problem!

The Quest Toolbox Series

This series is different. It provides practical techniques, tested by experienced consultants with real organisations. Each tool follows a step-by-step approach, illustrated by worked examples. No theoretical explanations, just a wide choice of techniques to help stimulate, drive and manage change and the people that create it. Hundreds of directors, managers and team leaders worldwide are already using the series for personal reference, as handout material for training programmes or as an aid for project or improvement teams.

Steve Smith

Dr Smith has been helping organisations transform their performance and culture for 20 years. His unique experience of witnessing and consulting in global corporate change has helped him become regarded as one of the most progressive change management consultants of his generation.

A regular speaker and author, as well as conceptual thinker, Steve has facilitated the metamorphosis of over 150 organisations through the provision of timely, supportive and often pioneering consultancy advice.

A strong advocate of an holistic approach to business improvement, Steve works with his clients to define stretching, yet balanced strategies that work, and then helps to mobilise the whole organisation to turn those strategies into action.

Prior to forming Quest, Steve was a director of PA Consulting Services, where he worked for 11 years and founded the TQM division. A former lecturer at Aston University, Steve has also spent eight years with the Chrysler Corporation.

Acknowledgements

The Toolbox series has been drawn from the expertise of the entire Quest Worldwide consultancy team. Special thanks must go to Gillian Hayward for selecting and compiling tools for all five titles and to Mike Rayburn who developed and refined many of the techniques in *Make Things Happen!* Thanks also to Peter Holman, Tina Jacobs, Sue Hodder and the Quest support team.

Solve That Problem!

Readymade Tools for Continuous Improvement

Edited by
Steve Smith

KOGAN PAGE

QUEST QUALITY

First South Asian Edition 1999
Reprinted 2005, 2009

Kogan Page India Private Limited
4737/23 Ansari Road,
Daryaganj
New Delhi 110 002

This edition is for sale in the Indian subcontinent only. Not for export elsewhere.

ISBN-10: 81-7554-100-8
ISBN-13: 978-81-7554-100-9

Published by Vinod Vasishtha for Kogan Page India Private Limited,
4737/23, Ansari Road, Daryaganj, New Delhi 110 002.

Printed and bound by Raj Press, R-3, Inderpuri, New Delhi - 110 012.

Contents

Introduction

The world's leading organisations continuously seek to improve their performance. There may be unlimited potential for achieving accelerated improvement but if this potential is not being realised, good change agents must line up and mobilise all the forces (or drivers) for improvement.

There are five main drivers for improvement in organisations:

- Strategy.
- Lean operations.
- Balanced culture.
- Customer responsiveness.
- Leadership.

Strategy sets direction and gives focus to improvement. It must however be deployed throughout the organisation to be effective.

Processes need to be mapped and analysed in a methodical way; projects must be managed; problem symptoms traced to root causes; data must be collected before decisions are taken; trends in customer preferences detected and fed back; improvement activity of any kind reported on and coordinated; improvement action measured. Just about everything should be done to a discipline.

A balanced culture means effective, creative management of people. Customers are served by people; processes are managed by people. Only people can deliver quality improvement. For them to work well they must be empowered, given direction, measured, reviewed and success recognised.

Customer responsiveness keeps the organisation focused on customer needs; reactions and changing requirements.

Finally, leadership ensures that everyone is enthused and supported to work on the strategy, improve processes, serve customers and be active team players.

Solve that problem! provides a quick reference guide to many of the tools and techniques which ensure a disciplined approach to continuous improvement.

How to use this Toolbox

This Toolbox contains a range of simple, practical tools which you can use as an individual or as a team to help you achieve effective results.

The Toolbox is divided into the main stages of the improvement process:

- Defining requirements and identifying the problem
- Data gathering
- Problem or issue analysis
- Generating ideas and options
- Making decisions
- Planning for action.

For each tool, there is a description of:

- What it is
- How to use it
- How it helps

along with an example of its use.

The matrices on pages viii-x link the tools to three detailed processes:

- Making simple improvements.
- Making more complex process improvements.
- Policy Deployment.

Each matrix shows the best tools to use at each step.

How to use it

1. Identify which stage of the improvement process you are at.
2. Refer to the main contents index for the tools available to help you at this stage.
3. Browse through the alternatives available and decide which is the most appropriate given your specific need.
4. Follow the 'How to use it' instructions and use the tool.
5. You may also find it helpful to look at the matrices (page viii) which link the tools in sequence relating to the detailed steps of PLAN-DO-CHECK-ACT.

How it helps

Nearly all of the tools in this Toolbox are simple and easy to use. Their strengths are that they:

- give **structure** to what otherwise can be rambling and disorganised thought
- **save time** by focusing thoughts and efforts
- increase the likelihood of **full participation and involvement** of everyone in a team
- are **fun** and **interesting to use** and make things visual
- **ensure problems and issues are fully explored** and analysed before jumping to action so increasing the likelihood of implementing **solutions that stick**.

Tools index

Linking PDCA and tools for simple improvement

Phase	Steps of improvement cycle / Which tools to use	Action Plan	Asking Why	Brainstorming	Cause and Effect Analysis	Check Sheets	Consensus Reaching	Control Charts	Cost Benefit Analysis	Customer-Supplier Agreements	Data Display	Force Field Analysis	Pareto Analysis	Process Mapping	Time/Cost Analysis
PLAN	1. Select an opportunity for improvement			✔			✔						✔		
	2. Identify the customer's requirements									✔					
	3. Define the problem		✔				✔							✔	
	4. Collect data					✔		✔						✔	✔
	5. Analyse for root causes		✔	✔	✔								✔	✔	✔
	6. Find solution			✔			✔		✔					✔	
	7. Prepare plan to implement solution	✔				✔						✔			
DO	8. Implement solution	✔													
CHECK	9. Monitor results, evaluation against plan					✔		✔		✔	✔				
	10. Determine reasons for deviations		✔	✔	✔		✔					✔	✔	✔	
ACT	11. Take corrective action for deviations	✔													
	12. Standardise in the process – make a successful solution permanent	✔						✔			✔			✔	
	13. Reflect			✔			✔		✔						✔

Linking PDCA and tools for process improvement

	Steps of process / Which tools to use	Action Plan	Asking Why Five Times	Benchmarking	Brainstorming	Cause & Effect Analysis	Check Sheets	Consensus Reaching	Control Charts	Cost Benefit Analysis	Customer-Supplier Agreements	Data Display	Decision Charts	Force Field Analysis	Gantt Chart	Pareto Analysis	Performance Expectation Grid	Process Mapping	Time/Cost Analysis
PLAN	1. Define the process				✔														
	2. Specify the customer's requirements										✔						✔		
	3. Collect performance data						✔		✔			✔					✔	✔	
	4. Analyse the process		✔			✔										✔	✔		✔
	5a. Identify benchmarks	✔		✔	✔														
	5b. Identify step-by-step improvements				✔			✔		✔									
	5c. Identify breakthroughs			✔	✔			✔										✔	
	6. Evaluate alternatives							✔		✔									
	7a. Redesign the process																	✔	
	7b. Develop an implementation plan	✔			✔									✔	✔				
DO	8. Implement plan	✔													✔				
CHECK	9. Monitor performance evaluate against plan	✔																	
	10. Identify reasons for deviations	✔					✔						✔						
ACT	11. Take corrective action for deviations	✔																	
	12. Standardise the process – make a successful solution permanent	✔			✔						✔								
	13. Review	✔			✔					✔							✔		

Linking PDCA to Policy Deployment and tools

Steps of process improvement		Action Plan	Affinity Diagram	Arrow Diagram/Process Decision Programme Chart	Brainstorming	Cause & Effect Analysis	Flag Method	Gantt Chart	Matrix Diagram	Pareto Analysis	Planning Table	Priorities Grid	Process Improvement Priority Matrix	Relations Diagram	SWOT Analysis	Tree Diagram
PLAN	1. Define company mission		✓		✓											
	2. Formulate long and medium term business plan		✓											✓	✓	
	3. Identify breakthrough goals				✓							✓				
	4. Define the target(s) and the means				✓	✓			✓	✓	✓					✓
	5. Determine and set relevant measures				✓				✓		✓					
DO	6. Deploy breakthrough goals and measures	✓		✓	✓		✓		✓		✓		✓	✓		✓
	7. Implement						✓	✓	✓	✓						
CHECK	8. Monitor progress			✓				✓	✓			✓				
ACT	9. Prepare report on achievements and next year's issues		✓			✓		✓		✓	✓				✓	✓

1 Define requirements and identify the problem

Customer-Supplier Agreement

What it is

A Customer-Supplier Agreement (CSA) is a written document detailing:

- the needs of a customer (either internal or external)
- what the supplier can deliver
- what is to be done to improve the delivery of the customer requirements.

It is sometimes called a 'service level agreement'.

How to use it

1. **Decide on the customer-supplier relationship to be addressed**

   The two main players – the supplier of the output and the customer – should agree in principle that a CSA would improve their part of the Quality chain.

2. **Identify other interested parties**

   Make sure that all interested parties understand what is happening and are willing to 'buy in' to the CSA.

3. **Prepare for the meeting**

   The two main players should individually review their customer-supplier relationship to generate ideas on, for example, needs and improvement targets. Data can also be gathered to make the discussion more objective.

   A CSA checklist to help preparation is shown overleaf.

Agreement checklist

- ✔ Who are the customer and supplier?
- ✔ Are there other interested parties?
- ✔ What are the customer requirements?
- ✔ How are the outputs to be measured?
- ✔ How is customer feedback to be monitored?
- ✔ What are the respective responsibilities and actions of the customer and supplier to ensure the agreed output?

Other headings, (eg what to do in case of disagreement) may be added as appropriate.

4. CSA discussion

The main players (and other interested parties if appropriate) should meet to discuss and develop an agreement.

Aim to keep the draft as simple as possible. A pro forma is shown on the next page along with instructions on what to put in each box.

5. Trial period

The initial agreement should be for a trial period and amended as required at the end of this time.

6. Regular review

The CSA should then be reviewed on a regular basis by the main players in order to update needs and performance measures and identify actions to further improve the relationship.

CUSTOMER-SUPPLIER AGREEMENT: Pro forma

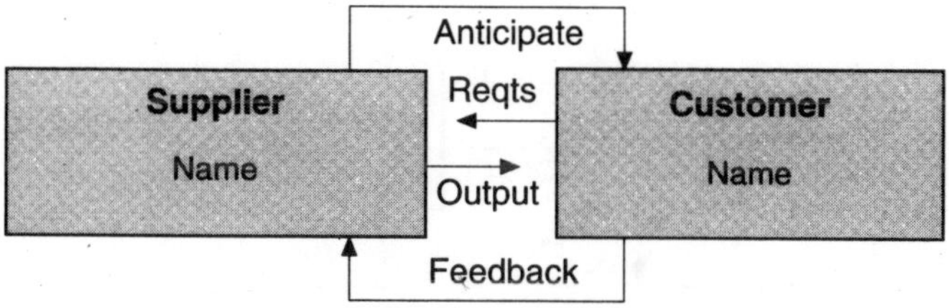

Supplier specification

Detailed standards, inputs and feedback the supplier needs to meet the customer's requirements

Customer requirements

What outputs the customer needs (these can be negotiated)

Measures	**Actual**	**Target**
Units of progress by which the supplier and customer will know if the needs are being met to the required standards	Current performance	Required performance

Improvement opportunities

All the areas for improvement in the current working relationship and practices

Agreed action	**By whom**	**By when**
Specific steps which either party will		
take to address the improvement		
opportunities		

Supplier Signature ______ **Date agreed** ______

Customer Signature ______ **Review date** ______
(to check if actions taken and performance improved)

CUSTOMER-SUPPLIER AGREEMENT: Example

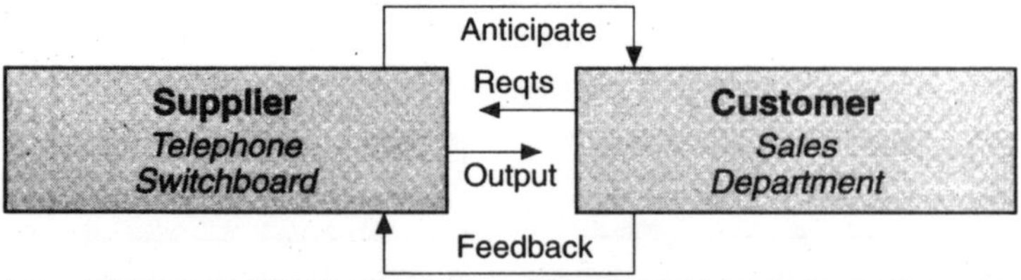

Supplier specification

To answer exchange calls within 20 seconds.
To establish nature of inquiry.
To transfer all external calls to the correct extension.

Customer requirements

To receive correct external calls from the switchboard.

Measures	Actual	Target
% calls answered after 20 seconds	*10%*	*0*
% calls transferred to incorrect extension	*20%*	*5%*

Improvement opportunities

- *Calls often transferred to the wrong extension, leading to external and internal customer frustration and delays.*
- *The directory entries are unclear, they confuse switchboard operators.*
- *The operators do not always find out the nature of the call and therefore put them through to the wrong extension.*

Agreed action	By whom	By when
1. *Sales Department to advise switchboard of correct extension numbers to use.*	*Sales Manager*	*End of week*
2. *Switchboard to obtain all relevant information from customers before transferring the call.*	*Switchboard Supervisor*	*Immediately*

Supplier *Switchboard Supervisor* **Date agreed** *22 December*
Customer *Sales Manager* **Review date** *31 January*

How it helps

A CSA can help ensure that the expectations of both customer and supplier are matched and highlight the elements which are key to maintaining or achieving the agreed output. It fosters teamwork between different departments and individuals.

REMEMBER, THE PURPOSE IS TO MAKE IMPROVEMENTS IN ORDER TO STRENGTHEN CUSTOMER SUPPLIER LINKS AND NOT TO GENERATE PAPER

CSAs can become extremely complicated – often it is best to start with a simple letter of understanding and add to it as problems are exposed.

CSAs can also become overly bureaucratic. It is important that they are focused on the areas of greatest need and paperwork is kept to a minimum.

Perception of Performance (POP) Graph

What it is

A Perception of Performance (POP) Graph is a graphical way of assessing performance against a Customer-Supplier Agreement.

How to use it

1. Work with your customer to identify the critical success factors in a particular transaction or relationship; focus on specific behaviours and measurable standards.
2. Plot these along the base axis.
3. At regular intervals, each party assesses how well the other has performed against the relevant factors and judges their own performance as appropriate.
4. A score is then assigned to each factor; 10 is excellent – 1 is unacceptable. These are then plotted on the graphs.
5. Meet to share perceptions, give feedback and identify actions. Focus first on the main gaps in order to reach a common understanding of actual performance and then on the areas of greatest shortfall.
6. Develop an action plan to address these areas for improvement.

For example:

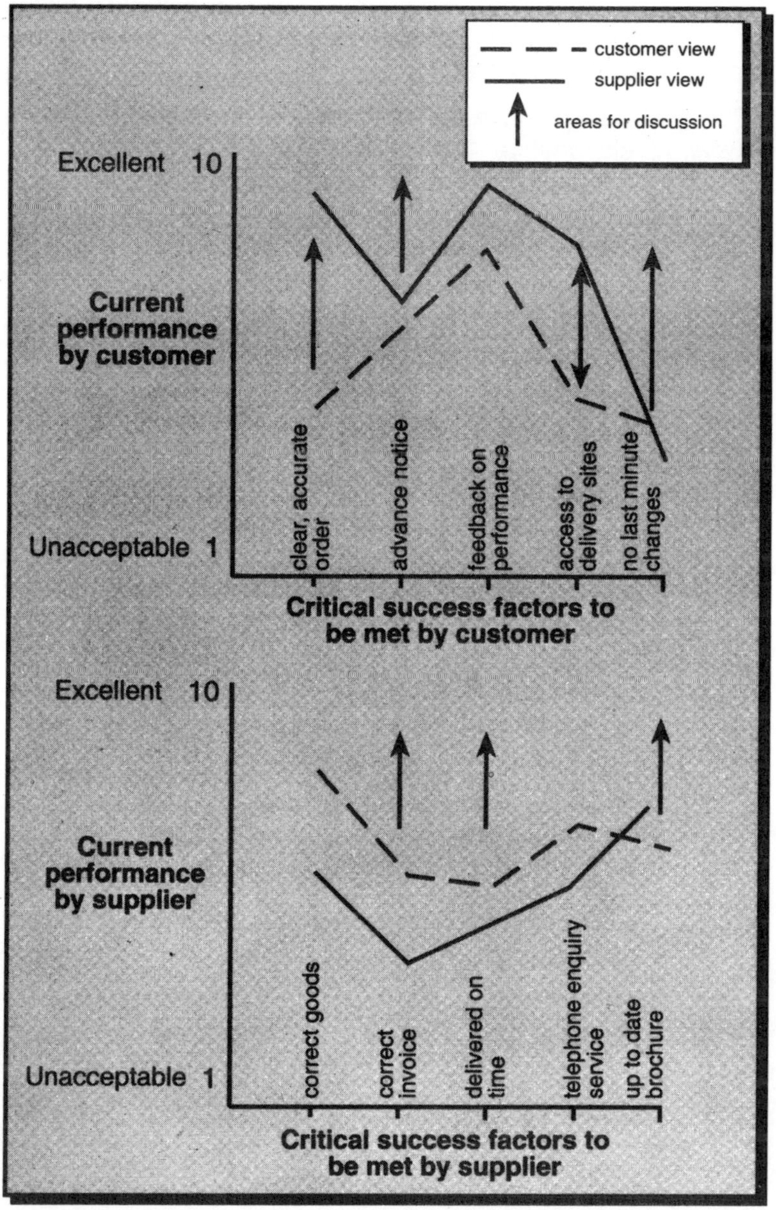
customer view
supplier view
areas for discussion
Excellent 10
Current performance by customer
Unacceptable 1
clear, accurate order
advance notice
feedback on performance
access to delivery sites
no last minute changes
Critical success factors to be met by customer
Excellent 10
Current performance by supplier
Unacceptable 1
correct goods
correct invoice
delivered on time
telephone enquiry service
up to date brochure
Critical success factors to be met by supplier

How it helps

A POP helps customers and suppliers work together to gain a common understanding of specific needs, current performance and areas for improvement.

A POP graph emphasises that both parties have a part to play in a two-way relationship.

Performance Expectation Grid

What it is

A Performance Expectation Grid pulls together key customer requirements and current performance in order to identify priority areas for improvement.

How to use it

1. Identify the key elements of performance which your customer requires and the standards they expect. Enter in the left hand column of the grid.
2. Identify the individual/departments/locations involved in delivering each element. Enter across the top row.
3. For each party and against each element identify current performance/contribution and enter in the bottom right of the appropriate box.
4. Identify what performance is required from each party in order to meet customer expectations and enter in the top left of the appropriate box.
5. Identify the most significant gaps in performance.
6. If helpful, repeat the process to expand on the apparent area for improvement.
7. Use other tools to understand the reasons for the performance gap(s) and develop action plans to tackle them.

For example: making clothes

	Customer expectation	Sales	Production	Warehouse	Delivery	Accounts
		Parties involved				
Accuracy	100%	100% / 95%	100% / 70%	100% / 99%	100% / 97%	100% / 80%
Completeness	100%	100% / 91%	100% / 65%	100% / 97%	100% / 94%	100% / 98%
Competitive price	Costs ≤£5 unit	£0.25 / £0.20	£3.00 / £4.00	£0.25 / £0.30	£1.00 / £0.50	£0.50 / £1.00
Delivery time	5 days	1 day / 1 day	1 day / 3 days	1 day / 2 days	1 day / 1 day	1 day / 1 day

Expand for area with most significant gaps

(required / current)

		Cutting	Sewing	Finishing
Accuracy	100%	100% / 80%	100% / 88%	100% / 91%
Completeness	100%	100% / 73%	100% / 94%	100% / 83%
Competitive price	Costs ≤£3 unit	£2.00 / £2.90	£0.70 / £0.80	£0.30 / £0.30
Delivery time	1 day	½day / 2½days	¼day / ¼day	¼day / ¼day

Further analysis

How it helps

A Performance Expectation Grid is a systematic way of relating external customer requirements to internal performance standards in order to identify priority areas for improvement.

Process Improvement Priority Matrix

What it is

A Process Improvement Priority Matrix (PIPM) is a simple technique for identifying the key processes which must be improved if the principal improvement objectives and, ultimately, the organisation's mission, are to be achieved.

How to use it

1. Identify the principal improvement objectives of the organisation.
2. Identify all the key processes within the organisation (avoid getting too detailed at this stage).
3. Organise the objectives and key processes in a matrix.
4. Identify the processes which will impact the most on achieving the objectives, ie those whose performance to a high standard is critical. (Be rigorous, otherwise you will not be able to differentiate between processes).
5. Check that you have identified all of the key processes by asking yourself – "If all the processes identified so far perform to a high standard, will the breakthrough be achieved?"
6. Add up the number of times each process has been ticked and enter this result in the matrix.
7. Assess the current performance of the process using the following scale:

Rating process performance level

1 = extremely high standard; improvement not necessary

2 = high standard; some improvement desirable

3 = acceptable standard; some improvement desirable

4 = below acceptable standard; improvement essential

5 = well below acceptable standard; substantial improvement essential.

Enter your chosen rating in the appropriate column.

	Principal improvement objectives								
Key processes	Improve customer service	Broaden product range	Improve supplier management	Improve management development	Professionalise marketing	No of times identified	Process performance rating	Overall score	Rank
Manufacturing	✓	✓		✓		3	4	12	3
Purchasing	✓		✓	✓		3	2	6	6=
Systems development		✓			✓	2	2	4	9=
Forecasting	✓	✓	✓		✓	4	4	16	2
Training	✓	✓			✓	4	3	12	3=
Marketing	✓				✓	2	3	6	6=
Recruitment	✓	✓		✓	✓	4	2	8	5
Budgeting	✓		✓	✓	✓	4	1	4	9=
New product development	✓	✓	✓		✓	4	5	20	1
Selling	✓	✓				2	3	6	6=

8. Now multiply the number of ticks by the rating and enter the overall score in the penultimate column. This scale indicates the relative importance of improving each process.

9. Finally, rank order the processes, highest first, and enter this in the final column.

10. Use process mapping and other tools to help you identify and plan improvements to the priority processes.

How it helps

PIPM has three main benefits:

- It is an effective means of identifying weak processes whose performance could seriously hamper or prevent the achievement of principal improvement objectives.
- It enables an order of priority to be set for allocating resources to improving processes.
- It can help to unite a management team in support of agreed priorities.

Team Purpose Analysis

What it is

Team Purpose Analysis is a process which helps a team or unit:

- define its purpose and align with the business strategy and goals
- define the requirements, measurements and working relationships with its customers and suppliers
- identify its key processes and performance measures
- carry out an activity/task analysis to show what is currently being done and why
- identify whether or not each activity meets specific customer requirements and is right first time
- make immediate gains
- identify improvement projects for action.

In doing so, it introduces structure and priority to the improvement process within a work team so focusing and maintaining energy.

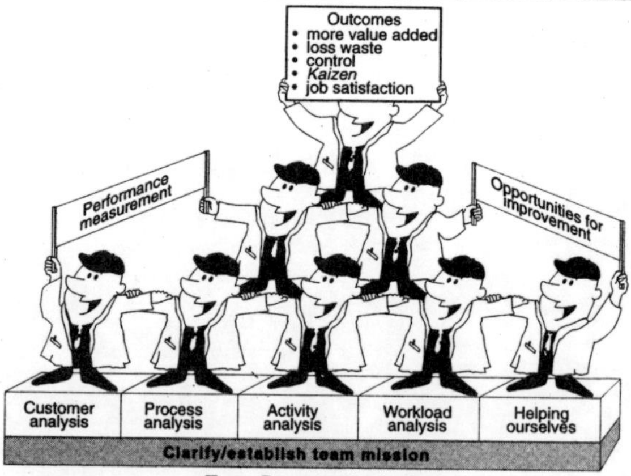

Team Purpose Analysis

Team purpose analysis (also known as departmental purpose analysis) brings together some improvement techniques to focus on what a team is doing and how it can do better. The important element is that the team does all the analysis (with the help of a facilitator at first). It can be very motivating and provides good outcomes.

How to use it

Over several months a team works through all or some of eight steps (depending on needs and priorities) addressing the following questions at each step:

1. **Clarify/establish team mission**
   - What is the overall mission and what are the goals of the organisation?
   - What is our contribution or role in achieving this mission?
   - What are our overall responsibilities and main outputs?
   - So what is our team mission?
2. **Review customers and suppliers**
   - Who are our customers/suppliers?
   - What are their/our requirements?
   - What is our/their current performance?
   - What measures/feedback mechanisms exist?
   - How can outputs/inputs/measures be improved?
3. **Review processes**
   - What are our key processes?
   - Are they mapped?
   - Are our performance measures adequate?
   - How can our processes be improved?
4. **Detailed activity analysis (on key processes to be improved)**
   - How long do they take?
   - How much do they cost?
   - Where is the waste?
   - How often do things happen/go wrong?

- How well do we use our resources?
- Do effort and results seem in balance?
- What should we start/stop/do differently?

5. Workload management analysis

- What are our workload volumes?
- What are the daily/weekly/monthly/annual variations and trends?
- How well do we predict and/or manage variation?
- How well do we balance workload and resource?
- How can we improve our workload management?

6. Helping ourselves (internal processes)

- Are our individual roles/responsibilities sufficiently clear and coordinated?
- How well do we document our procedures and record our work?
- Do we meet our training needs sufficiently well?
- How well do we communicate with each other?
- How could we improve our teamworking?

7. Performance measures

Taking into account topics 1-6:

- What are our overall performance measures?
- Is sufficient, timely information available on these to take prompt action?

8. Opportunities for improvement

- What is the range of opportunities?
- What is urgent?
- How do we fix it?

- Can we make step by step improvements?
- Why can't we just "do it"?
- What is in most need of a radical breakthrough improvement?
- Where do we need to use a project team?
- Do we need to benchmark ourselves?
- How shall we prioritise the bigger issues?
- Who is going to do what?
- How will we review our progress?

HINT! YOU DON'T HAVE TO COMPLETE 1-7 BEFORE DOING SOME OF 8!

The Overall Process

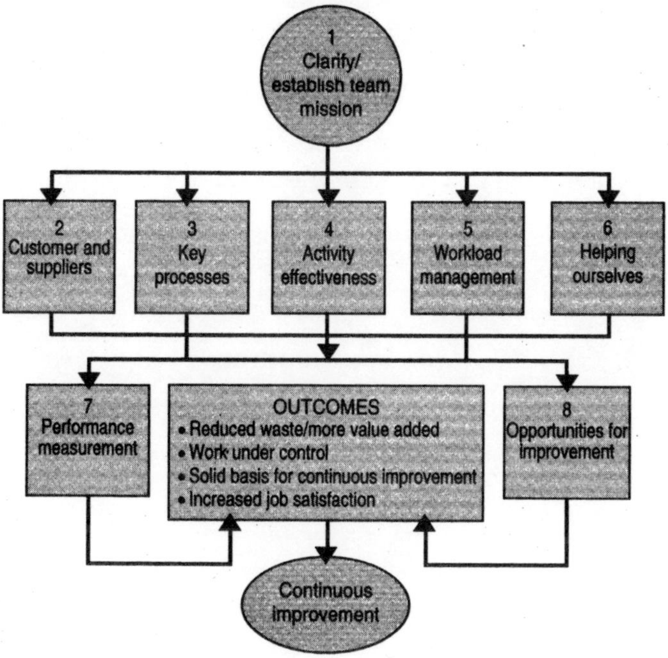

How it helps

Team Purpose Analysis helps a team focus, prioritise and organise improvement activity. It helps to ensure that customer requirements are met, processes are managed, waste is removed and the team works effectively together. Unlike all of the other tools, which take minutes or hours, TPA is an ongoing process over many months.

2 Gather data

Affinity Diagram (or K J Method)

(developed by Mr Jiro Kawakita)

What it is

The KJ Method is a technique for capturing all the views, ideas and responses to particular issues including emotional and behavioural aspects. Affinity diagrams order this verbal data by collating them into similar categories so that they can be analysed.

How to use It

1. Select an issue. This does not need to be so precisely expressed as it does for conventional problem-solving.
2. Individually identify ideas/concerns/feelings about the issue. Emotional and behavioural ideas and reactions should be encouraged as well as rational and intellectual ones.
3. Ask each individual to write their views on individual cards or Post-it® Notes.

> HINT!
>
> SEEK VOLUME – AT THIS STAGE 50 PLUS IS USUAL

4. Silently, as a team, sort the cards by grouping together similar items on the basis of their affinity. Don't just use reason, use feelings too. You should 'feel' that the cards belong together. Repeat this process until clear groupings are formed. Cards which are 'strange' or inappropriately filed should be taken out of the group and returned to the pre-sorting file.

Cards which do not fit into any of the groups should be isolated and left to one side. Continue this sorting process until everyone is happy with the groupings. It is common to end up with 5-10 groupings.

5. Construct the affinity diagram from the cards and reach consensus on a title for each grouping. If appropriate, break each grouping into sub-sections with titles.

6. In presenting the data expect to use phrases like: "we feel...", "our impression is...", "it appears...".

7. Consider using Consensus Reaching as a way of identifying priorities for action.

For example:

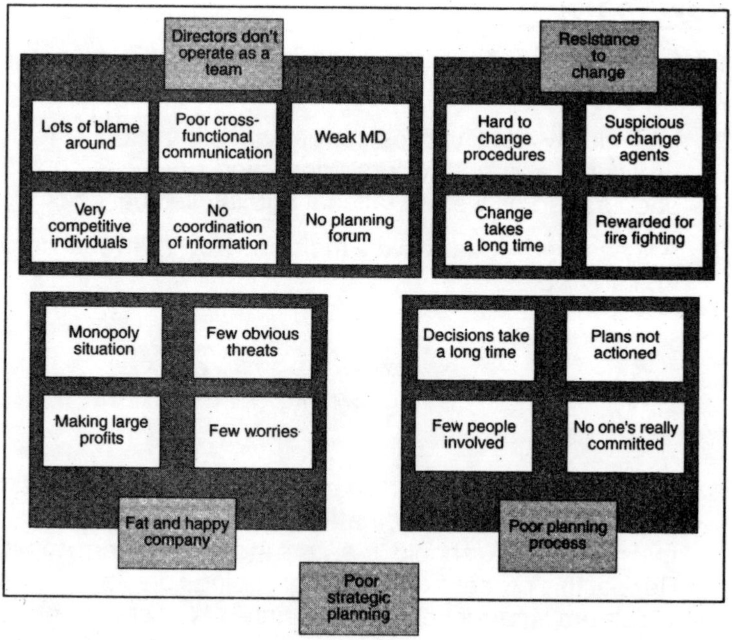

How it helps

An Affinity Diagram is a simple way of processing the subjective/emotional/perceptual data which we all carry and can often give vital clues to the real root cause/solution in a problem. Like many tools it is simply a vehicle for discussion and involvement to be used in parallel with tools which focus more on facts and numerical data.

In effect it is a less structured form of Cause and Effect Analysis.

Check Sheet

What it is

A Check Sheet is a way of collecting and classifying information so that it can be easily presented or analysed. It is particularly useful at the start of a problem-solving process for data gathering but also for monitoring performance once change has been implemented.

No matter how simple or complex the Check Sheet, the principle is the same.

How to use it

1. **Specify the objective of the *Check Sheet***

   Decide why the facts are required. For example: to determine reasons for increasing levels of credit notes.

2. **Agree the information to be collected**

   Decide the types of data required and how it will be classified. For example: customer, order number, nature of complaint, date, driver. Ensure data can be broken into subgroups/ classes if there are likely to be differences. For example: by depot or customer type.

3. **Identify appropriate timescales**

   Decide over what period the data will be collected – hours? days? weeks? months? At what intervals will the data be taken if it is on a sample basis; once an hour? every tenth batch/customer? random? For example: all credit notes for four weeks. using daily driver returns.

4. **Decide who will collect the data**

   Identify the most appropriate individuals to collect the data. Ensure they have the time and information to do so accurately.

5. Design the *Check Sheet*

Prepare an initial design. Ensure it is clear, complete and easy to use.

6. Trial the *Check Sheet*

Agree who will try out the check sheet. After an appropriate period, review the format, categories and sample numbers/ times and update as appropriate. Make sure that everyone collecting the facts understands the meaning of the classifications. Go back to Step 2 if necessary.

7. Collect the data

The people collecting the facts should ideally be those included in the problem – not advisors, consultants or inspectors! Check however, that everyone is clear about what they are doing and that the exercise is being applied consistently and accurately.

8. Analyse the data

Use Data Display and/or Pareto Analysis to highlight main patterns, trends and issues.

For example:

Credit note check sheet		
Driver: Fred		**Date:** 1 June
Order no	**Customer name**	**Reason for credit note**
13427	Jo's Cafe	Wrong pack of frozen chips
65021	Newtown High School	Split 25lb bag of flour
32967	Miller Industrial	Missing 5 dozen eggs
45631	Resteasy Retirement Home	Wanted 10 not 100 packs of incontinence pads
29438	Upmarket Restaurant	Returned 'inedible' pastry mix

Once completed these Check Sheets would be analysed to categorise reasons for credit notes.

For example:

Main reasons for credit notes issued	Number issued
Product damage (packaging)	50
Product quality (manufacturing)	34
Missing items	10
Wrong quality	6
Wrong pack size	5
Wrong brand	3

9. Use other tools as appropriate to identify the next steps

Once the main category(s) is identified, Cause and Effect Analysis could be used to analyse why this keeps recurring.

How it helps

Facts are better than opinions. The *Check Sheet* allows facts about a problem to be established at source. The facts can then be subjected to Pareto Analysis/Cause and Effect Analysis, before actions are agreed.

Control Charts

What it is

Variation is inherent in everything we do. A Control Chart is a graph for monitoring the variation in a process or activity, which has superimposed alert indicators. The alert indicators are not guessed but are calculated using statistical theories of probability. As soon as performance approaches or crosses the action lines, steps should be taken to investigate this variation in order to correct it and remove the source. Over a period of time, these reactive actions, if investigated and standardised, improve the capability of the process and so reduce the likelihood of failure to meet requirements.

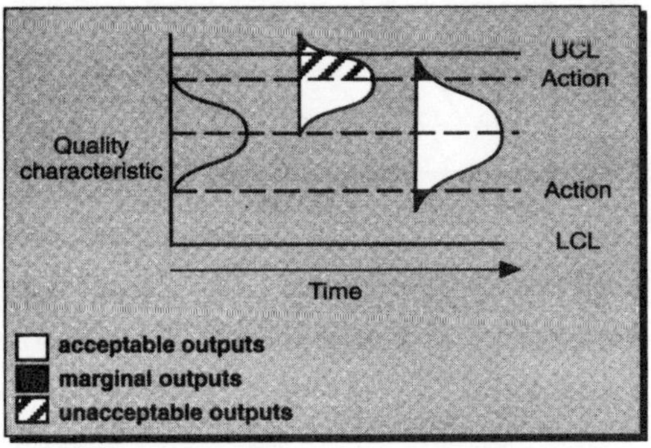

How to use it

Control Charts were originally developed to monitor manufacturing processes, but have been found helpful throughout an organisation. The details of how to develop a control chart are beyond the scope of this Toolbox as they involve the analysis of frequency distributions and the calculation of standard deviations.

Control charts are valuable since if a process changes and the change were to go undetected, there is a danger of not meeting the customer's requirements. The alert indicators, sometimes called 'action lines', clearly define when action (which may be STOP), should be taken. They are usually set within the control limits so that action is taken before outputs become unacceptable. The control limits are set at the required number of standard deviations either side of the mean. Because the limits clearly define the expected behaviours of the process, they can also help to prevent unnecessary intervention.

For example:

How it helps

The Control Chart enables a process to be monitored between

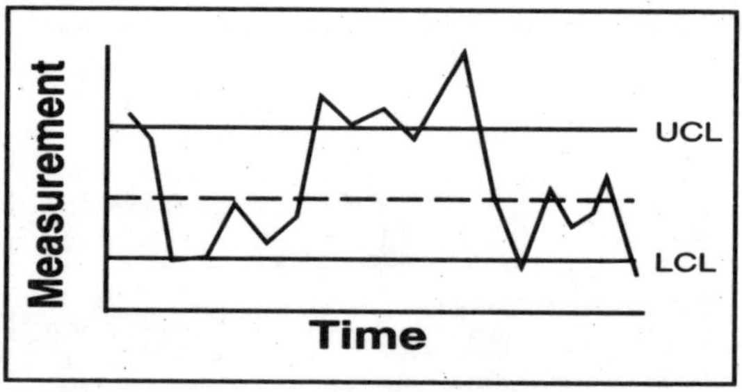

preset limits so that action can take place if the data shows that either the 'action lines' or 'control limits' are breached.

Data Display

What it is

Data display, as the name suggests, are different methods of displaying information in order to make it easy to use, to highlight patterns, trends and relationships and make data more interesting for a wider population. The main types of charts are:

- bar charts
- histograms
- pie charts
- scatter diagrams
- run (trend) graphs
- spider diagrams.

The patterns, trends or relationships you wish to show will determine which of the above you choose.

How to use it

Bar chart

This display tool enables comparison of several discrete items with each other.

For example: average sales at a greengrocers (over a three month period)

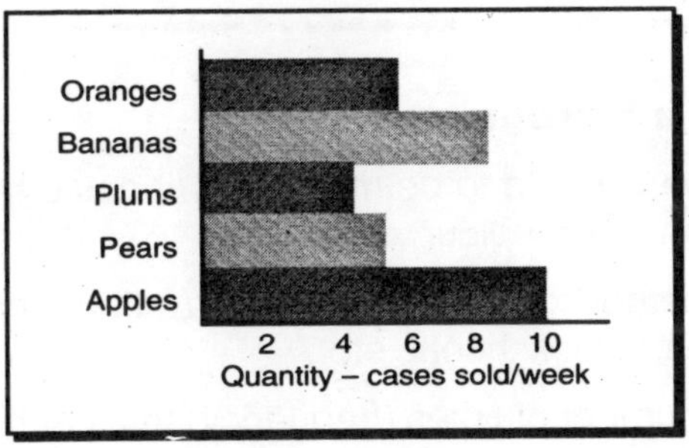

To develop a bar chart:

1. Identify the items to be measured.
2. Design a method for collecting the data (including sampling, time frames, check sheets as needed).
3. Review the data collected and decide on a suitable horizontal scale.
4. Plot items up the vertical scale.
5. Draw in bars to show the different quantities/performances/ values, etc of each item.

Histogram

A Histogram shows the range of data which has been collected on a particular process or characteristic. It shows the frequency distribution in bar form. The data used in histograms is also the starting point for developing control charts as it is linked to variation.

For example:

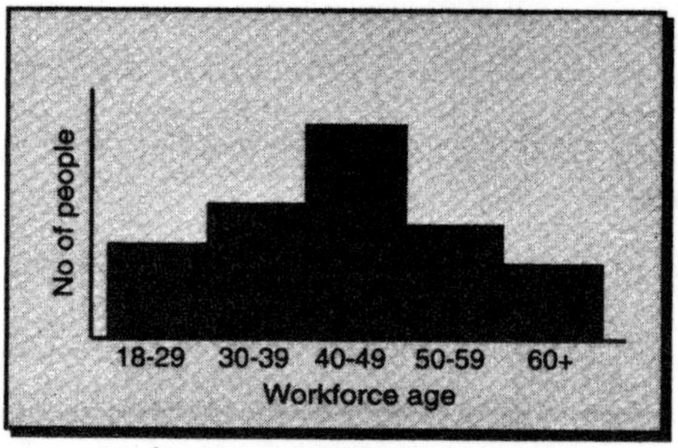

To develop a histogram:

1. Identify the variable to be measured (it could be age, size, satisfaction, cost, colour, etc).
2. Set up a method to collect information (categories, sampling, timeframes, checksheets, etc).
3. Total the number of times (frequency) that each category of the variable has occurred.

4. Break the horizontal axis into sections for each category.
5. Choose a suitable scale for the vertical axis given the frequency distribution.
6. Plot the bars for each category.

Pie charts

This display tool shows proportions in relation to the whole item. It has visual impact and also allows easy, visual comparison with other pie charts when percentages are used.

For example: sources of company profit

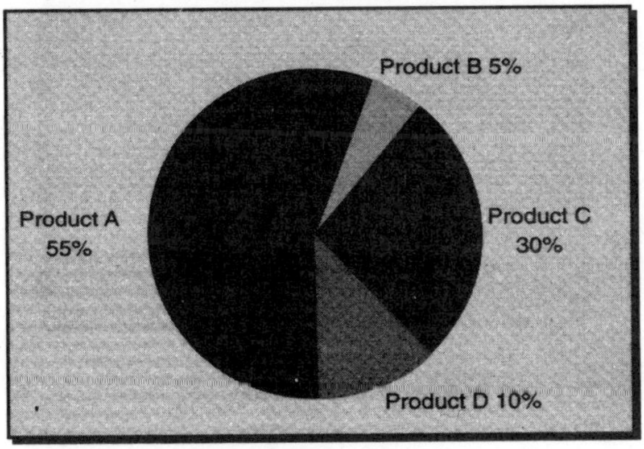

To develop a pie chart:

1. Identify the item to be measured and the appropriate subdivisions.
2. Collect data on the total performance (no. people, products, money, rejects, satisfaction ratings, etc).
3. Identify how this is broken down across the subdivisions already identified.

4. Turn the total and subdivisions into percentages.
5. Break up the pie chart in proportion to these percentages and label clearly.

Scatter diagram

This display tool identifies relationships between two variables by plotting changes in both.

For example: the relationship between advertising and sales volumes

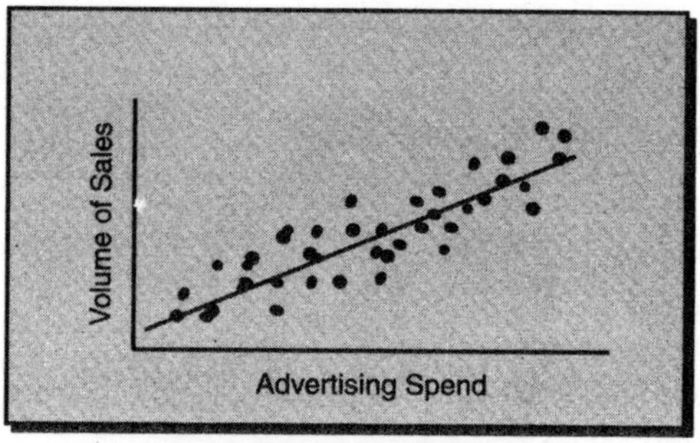

To develop a scatter diagram:

1. Identify the two variables to be considered.
2. Devise a method of collecting performance data on both over, eg time/sites/individuals/products.
3. Plot suitable scales on each axis. While it is wrong to jump immediately to a cause and effect relationship, plot the more likely cause or driver on the horizontal axis.
4. Plot each pair of measures on the graph.
5. The more closely the dots are aligned, the stronger the correlation (positive or negative) between the two. A random pattern of dots means there is no relationship.

Run (Trend) chart

(sometimes called a line graph)

This display tool is used to display trends in one variable over time.

For example: overall sickness rates in a unit

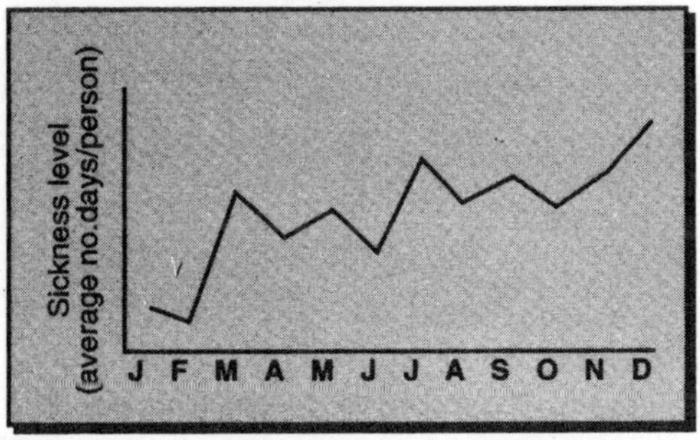

To develop a run chart:

1. Identify the variable to be measured.
2. Develop a method of data collection (timeframes, definitions, who collects, etc).
3. Draw the axes on suitable scales given the overall time frame and range of likely performance.
4. Plot each measure either retrospectively or allow the graph to build over time as the data becomes available.

Spider diagram

A spider diagram is a way of showing performance on a range of dimensions each of which is a component of an overall issue.

For example: leadership performance

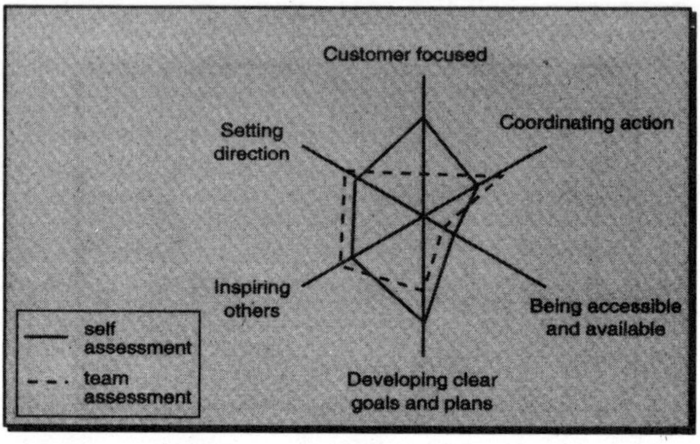

To develop a spider diagram:

1. Identify the issue to be measured and its component parts.
2. Develop a method of collecting data which will allow the information to be plotted on linear scales.
3. Collect the data.
4. Collate the data and summarise the performance of each component on a common scale, (eg percentages, dimensions, cost, ratings, etc).
5. Draw a spider diagram with the appropriate number of 'legs' and add the same scale to each.
6. Plot the performance of each component and label clearly.
7. If appropriate add previous performance/targets/benchmarks for comparison.

How it helps

Data Display helps demonstrate relationships, patterns and trends in data. The methods available are visual, interesting and easier to use than tables of raw data. They help to turn raw data into usable information.

Process Mapping

What it is

A Process Map is a pictorial representation of a process, using basic flowcharting symbols.

How to use it

The basic symbols are:

1. Identify your key processes

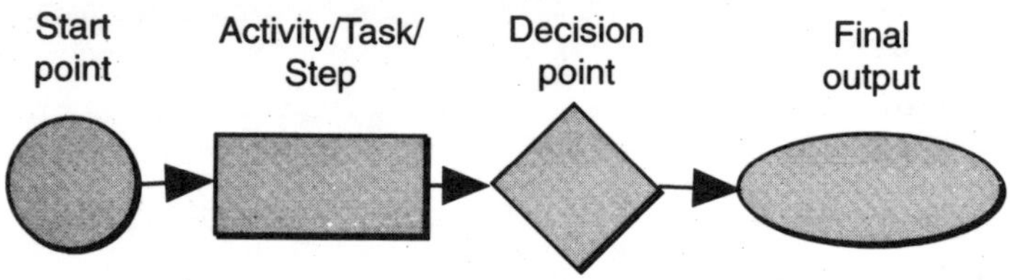

> **HINT!** KEEP FOCUSED ON THE OVERALL PURPOSE OF THE PROCESS OTHERWISE CHANGES MAY NOT ACHIEVE REAL IMPROVEMENT

These should:

- be large enough to count in terms of delivering the agreed output
- be small enough to map and understand
- result in output which is aimed at meeting the requirements of a customer.

Processes can involve many disciplines, eg developing a new product would require contributions from R&D, marketing, manufacturing, or be restricted to a specific area, eg, updating a computer printout. The one(s) you choose to focus on will depend on your position and level in the organisation.

> **HINT!** SETTING CLEAR, AGREED BOUNDARIES IS VITAL – KEEP IT SIMPLE

2. Establish a process team

Assemble people as a team who between them know the full range of activities making up the process. The team may range from a senior management group to a small number of people with similar duties.

Agree who the Process Owner or leader should be.

3. Set the boundaries of the process

Agree where you will start and stop for the purposes of the exercise. Choose natural break points.

4. Determine appropriate level of detail

Determine the level of detail appropriate to your improvement work. Should it be fine detail or 'the big picture'?

5. Identify all activities that make up the process

Brainstorm all the activities that make up the process. Put all ideas onto individual 'Post -it®'Notes. This makes it easier to move them around later. Describe each activity as a noun and verb, eg 'report written'.

A simple inputs/outputs diagram can be used prior to brainstorming to help identify both the key inputs and outputs for a process and the secondary information flows in and out of the process. This helps everyone to consider the whole process when brainstorming.

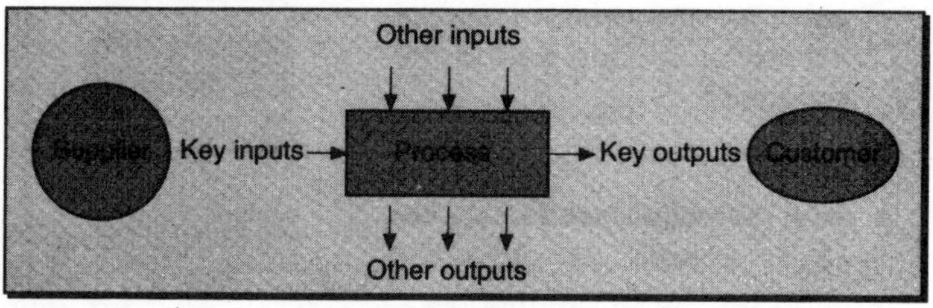

HINT!

BEWARE OF MUDDLING UP THE CURRENT AND IDEAL PROCESSES

6. Sequence the process activities

Use 'Post-it®' Notes to establish the correct sequence of activities.

7. Show decision points and connections between the activities

8. Conduct a TOPIC analysis

Consider where in the process map you can add information under the following categories:

Time:

- actual time (how long does the activity take?)
- elapsed time (how long before another task must the activity be performed?)

Ownership:

- who is responsible for or influential in each part of the process?

Personnel:

- who actually carries out the task (name a specific individual or department)
- is it done right first time?

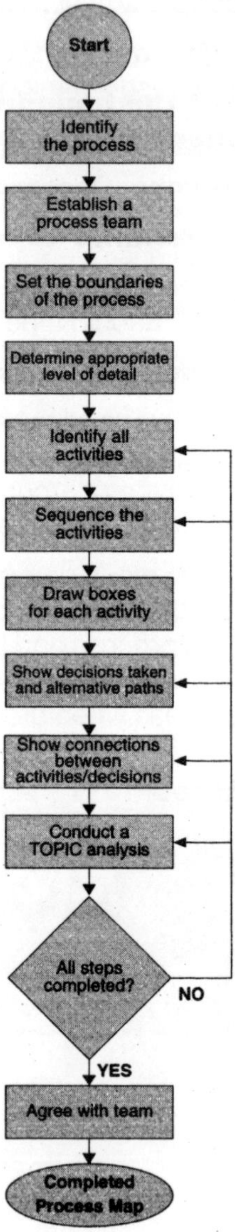

Information:

- what information is needed for/results from each step?
- Is any information lacking/superfluous?

Cost:

- what is the cost of each activity? How much of this cost is the result of things not being done 'right first time'.

9. Check for completeness

Ensure every activity is included, every box is connected, every decision point has at least two exits. Correct any omissions or errors.

10. Analyse the process

- Does the current process operate successfully?
- Challenge the complexity of the process. Can the process be simplified?
- Examine the value or benefit of each step. Are there clear Customer-Supplier Agreements?
- Where do errors and waste occur – how can they be avoided?
- Take a fresh look: 'why do we do it this way?'
- It may be necessary to collect further data using check sheets to complete the analysis.

11. Agree next steps

Agree Action Plans for improving the process.

For example:

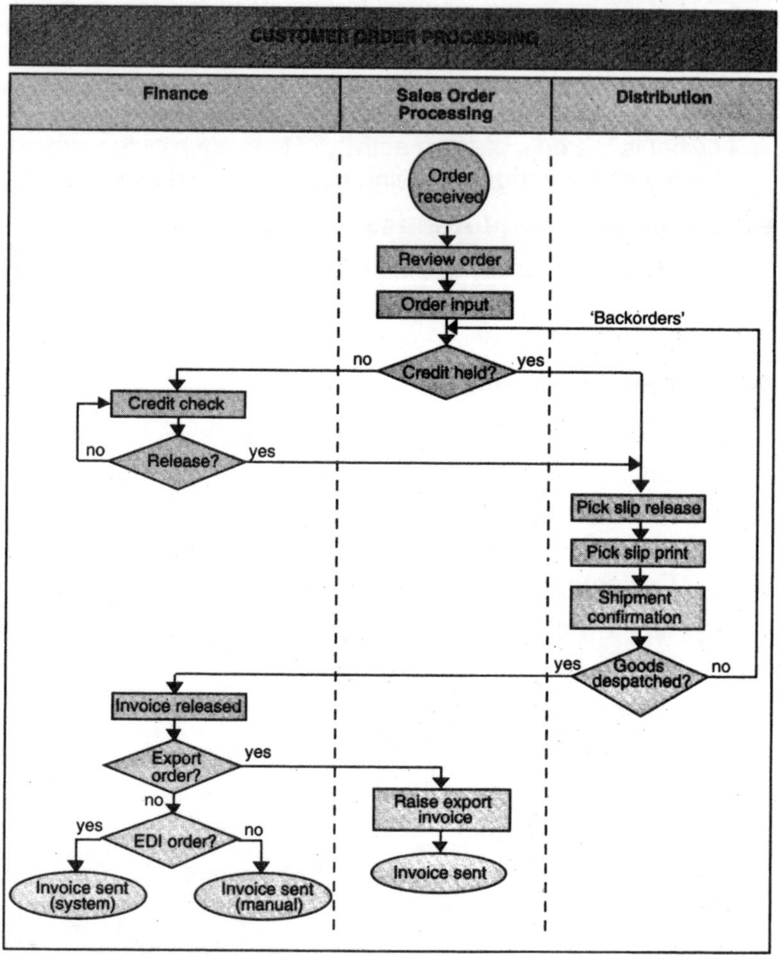

How it helps

Mapping helps you to:

- understand how a process currently operates
- manage how it currently operates
- identify and plan improvements.

Matrix Diagram

What it is

A matrix (or table) is a way of displaying large amounts of data. Matrices can also be used to show the presence or absence of relationships between pairs of elements/sets of data.

How to use it

1. Identify the data to be displayed.

2. Design an appropriate matrix format.

3. Indicate relationships between pairs of data (if this is the purpose of the matrix).

Goals

Key processes	A	B	C	D
1	●	□		●
2		○	●	
3		●	□	
4	●			
5	●			

Processes

Projects	1	2	3	4	5
A	□	●		●	○
B	○		○	□	
C		●	□	□	●
D		□		○	□
E	●	□	○	○	●

Symbols can be used to differentiate between strengths of relationship, eg
● = strong relationship, ○ = some relationship, □ = no relationship

The following page shows the use of a matrix to develop plans to improve a specific sporting breakthrough.

For example: goal – to improve golf

	Reduce putts to 1.75 per hole	Lengthen drive to 300 metres	Reduce iron shots to 1.25 per hole	Measures	Data	Frequency
Practice putting	●	□	□	practice puts per week	control chart	daily
Practice driving	□	●	○	practice drives per week	control chart	daily
Weight training	□	○	○	weights lifted progression	histo-grams	daily
Lessons with professional	○	●	●			
Measure	putts per week	estimated distance of drives	shots per hole			
Data	control chart	histo-grams	control chart			
Frequency	daily	daily	daily			

How it helps

Matrix Diagrams are an effective way of identifying priorities and relationships between variables and also of displaying large volumes of related information.

Time/Cost Analysis

What it is

Time/Cost Analysis is a graphical way of illustrating the relationship between the time taken to complete each stage of a process, the amount of cost added/invested in each stage and the overall cycle time.

How to use it

1. Identify the process to be analysed.
2. Use process mapping to identify the specific steps that make up the process.
3. For each step in the process, collect data on:
   - amount of time spent working at each step
   - the elapsed time of each step
   - the cost of each step (labour, materials, equipment, space, etc).

   If there is significant variation in the process, use a histogram to identify the average time or cost per unit/batch.
4. Plot cost against time for each step of the process on a graph.
5. Use this graph to question:
   - areas of high investment of time
   - areas of high added cost
   - the amount of active as opposed to waiting time for each activity as a basis for identifying process improvements.

For example: decorating a room (the DIY enthusiast's version!)

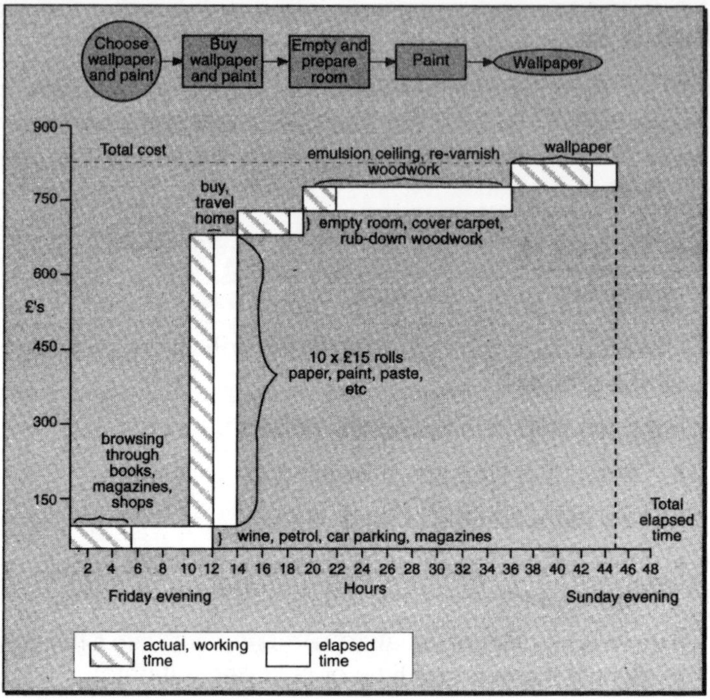

The goal of the analysis is to:

- reduce overall cycle time
- increase value-added more quickly by cutting out wasted time
- remove non-value adding steps.

How it helps

Time/Cost Analysis can be used to identify the areas of greatest opportunity (in terms of time and money) for process improvement.

3 Analyse the problem/issue

Asking Why Five Times

What it is

Asking Why is a simple technique used to analyse the causes of problems.

How to use it

Asking Why simply involves repeatedly asking 'why?' until the answer is 'because that's the way it is'. At this point, it is likely that you have identified a root cause of the problem. If tackled and removed, the observed symptoms of the problem should also disappear.

For example:

1. Why is there a high reject rate of widgets? Because the plastic is stained.
2. Why is the plastic stained? Because there is excess oil in the cutting machine.
3. Why is there excess oil in the cutting machine? Because it is clogging as it is months since it was cleaned.
4. Why is it so long since it was cleaned? Because we only service machines when they breakdown, not on a preventative basis.
5. Why only service after breakdowns? Because maintenance say it is cheaper (but what about the cost of rejects and rework?).

Although called 'Asking Why Five Times', five is a rule of thumb. There may be more or less questions depending on the particular situation. It is important to beware of channelling your analysis down one avenue and completely ignoring other root causes of the same problem.

How it helps

Asking Why is a way of identifying the underlying root cause of a problem so that this can be tackled rather than dealing only with superficial symptoms.

It should be seen as a simple and quick alternative to Cause and Effect Analysis.

Cause and Effect Analysis

What it is

Cause and Effect Analysis is a technique for identifying all the possible causes (inputs) associated with a particular problem/effect (output) before narrowing down to the small number of main, root causes which need to be addressed.

A Cause and Effect diagram (also known as a Fishbone or Ishikawa diagram) graphically illustrates the results of the analysis and is constructed in steps. Cause and Effect Analysis is usually carried out by a group who all have experience and knowledge of the cause to be analysed.

How to use it

1. Select the problem

Select a particular problem or effect.

Make sure the problem is specific, tightly defined and relatively small in scope and that everyone participating understands exactly what is being analysed.

Write the problem definition at the top of the flip chart or whiteboard.

2. Brainstorm

Conduct a Brainstorm of all the possible causes of the effect, ie problem.

Write each idea on a Post-it® to make it easy to transfer them onto the fishbone diagram later. Be careful not to muddle causes and solutions at this stage. It is important to brainstorm before identifying cause categories otherwise you can constrain the range of ideas. However, if ideas are slow in coming use questions such as, 'what about?', to prompt thoughts.

3. Draw fishbone diagram

Place the effect at the head of the fish

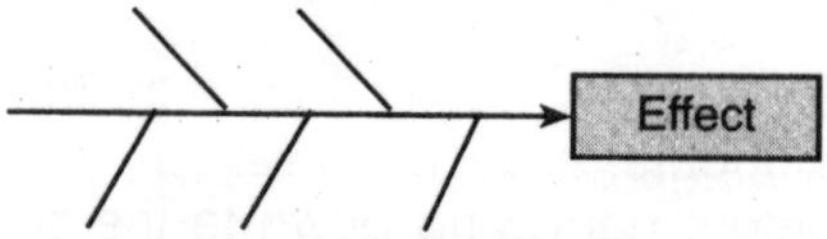

4. Establish cause categories

Review your brainstorm outputs to determine the major cause categories. Frequently used categories are:

- People
- Equipment
- Materials
- Environment (physical or cultural)
- Method or process.

These five do not fit every situation and different major categories might well be appropriate but should not exceed six.

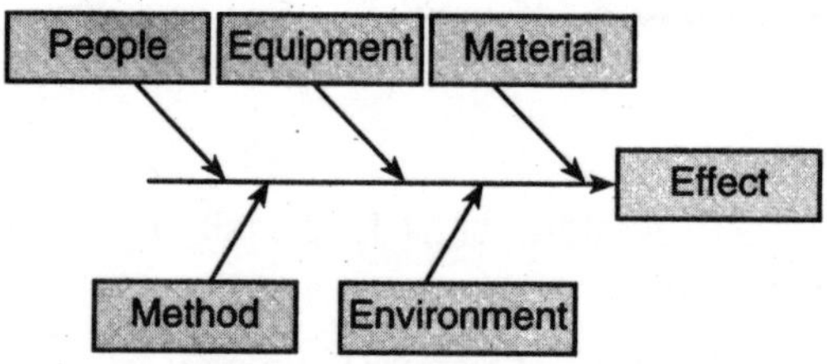

Other commonly used categories are:

- Communications
- Policies
- Measurement
- Customers/suppliers
- Systems, etc.

HINT! *THERE IS NO ONE PERFECT SET OF CATEGORIES. YOU MUST ADAPT TO SUIT THE ISSUE BEING ANALYSED*

5. Allocate causes

Transfer the potential causes from the brainstorm to the diagram, placing each cause under the appropriate category.

If causes seem to fit more than one category then it is acceptable to duplicate them. However, if this happens repeatedly it may be a clue that the categories are wrong and you should go back to step 4.

Related causes are plotted as 'twigs' on the branches.

Branches and twigs can be further developed by asking questions such as 'what?', 'why?' 'how?', 'where?' This avoids using broad statements which may in themselves be effects. Beware, however, of digging in and getting into bigger issues that are completely beyond the influence of the team.

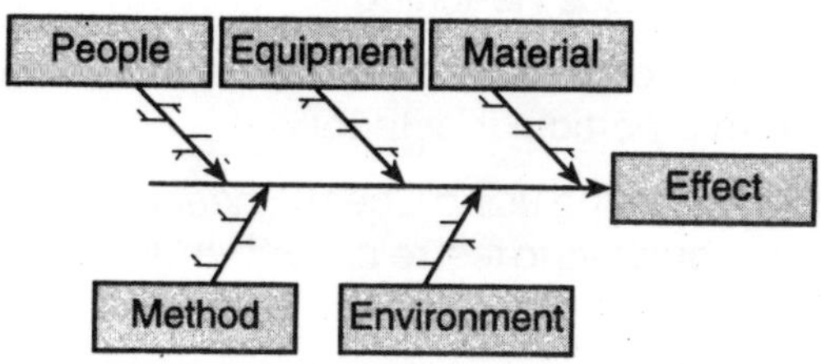

For example: broken lamp

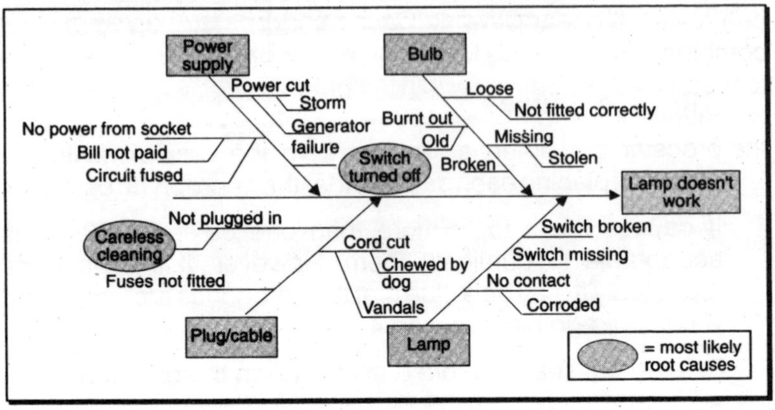

6. Analyse for root causes

Consider which are the most likely root causes of the effect. This can be done in several ways:

1. Through open discussion among participants, sharing views and experiences. This can be speeded up by using Consensus Reaching.
2. By looking for repeated causes or number of causes related to a particular category.
3. By data gathering using Check Sheets, Process Maps or customer surveys to test relative strengths through Pareto Analysis.
4. Once a relatively small number of main causes have been agreed upon, Paired Comparisons, can be used to narrow down further.
5. Some groups find it helpful to consider only those causes they can influence.

7. Test for reality

Test the most likely causes by, eg data gathering and observation if this has not already been done.

The diagram can be posted on a wall and added to/modified as further ideas are generated either by the team or by others who can review the teams' work. Cause and Effect Analysis can be combined with Process Mapping. A fishbone may be developed for each discrete activity within the process that is generating the output/effect so that causes are linked to particular steps in the process.

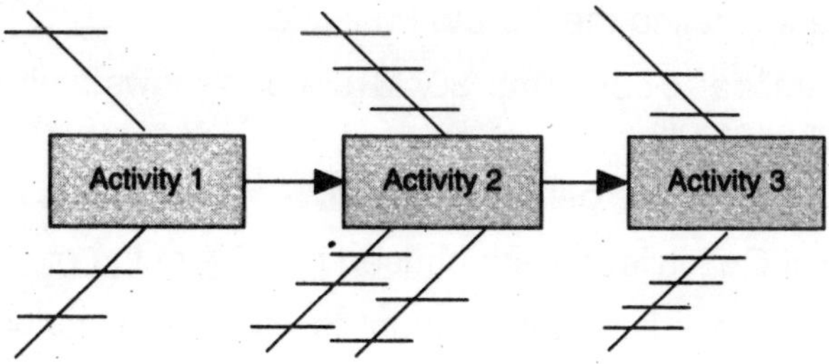

How it helps

Cause and Effect Analysis is a valuable tool for:

- focusing on causes not symptoms
- capturing the collective knowledge and experience of a group
- providing a picture of why an effect is happening
- establishing a sound basis for further data gathering and action.

Cause and Effect Analysis can also be used to identify all of the areas which need to be tackled to generate a positive effect.

Pareto Analysis

What it is

This technique is used to record and analyse data relating to a problem in such a way as to highlight the most significant areas, inputs or issues. Pareto Analysis often reveals that a small number of failures are responsible for the bulk of quality costs, a phenomenon called the 'Pareto Principle.'

This pattern is also called the '80/20 rule' and shows itself in many ways. For example:

- 80% of sales are generated by 20% of customers.
- 80% of Quality costs are caused by 20% of the problems.
- 20% of stock lines will account for 80% of the value of the stock.

A Pareto diagram allows data to be displayed as a bar chart and enables the main contributors to a problem to be highlighted.

How to use it

1. Gather facts about the problem, using Check Sheets or Brainstorming, depending on the availability of information.

For example: typing re-work

Reasons for typing re-work	No of times
Author errors	12
Incorrect entry	2
Poor layout	5
Improved content	15
Information became out of date	3

2. Rank the contributions to the problem in order of frequency.

Error	Frequency
Improved content	15
Authors errors	12
Poor layout	5
Information out of date	3
Incorrect entry	2
Total	37

3. Draw the value (errors, facts, etc) as a bar chart.

4. It can also be helpful to add a line showing the cumulative percentage of errors as each category is added. This helps to identify the categories contributing to 80% of the problem.

5. Review the chart – if an 80/20 combination is not obvious, you may need to redefine your classifications and go back to Stage 1 or 2.

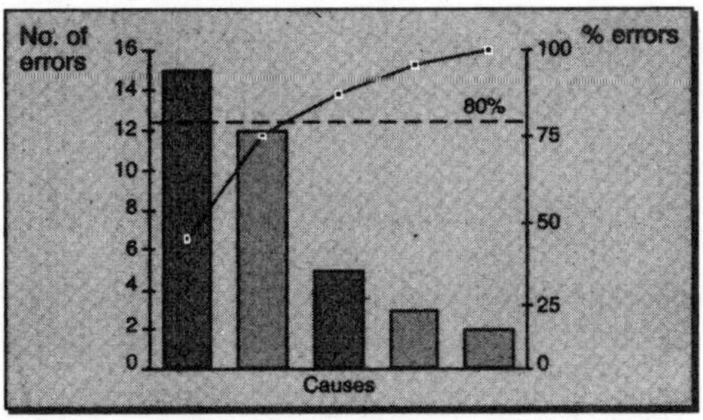

How it helps

Pareto Analysis is a useful tool to:

- identify and prioritise major problem areas
- separate the 'vital few' from the 'useful many' things to do
- identify major causes and effects.

The technique is often used in conjunction with Brainstorming and Cause and Effect Analysis.

> **HINT!** THE MOST FREQUENT IS NOT ALWAYS THE MOST IMPORTANT. BE AWARE OF THE IMPACT OF OTHER CAUSES ON CUSTOMERS OR GOALS

Relations Diagram

What it is

A Relations Diagram is a technique to relate complex cause and effect relationships. While there are clearly similarities with Fishbone Diagrams and Asking Why, Relations Diagrams allow you to investigate the multiple chains of effects and causes which often exist and to illustrate these graphically.

How to use it

1. Define the effect to be analysed or created. Write this in the middle of your board.
2. 'Ask Why' to identify the key factors which cause this effect. Write these as the main spokes off the effect.
3. In turn, look at each cause as an effect in its own right and identify further causes by again asking why. Add these to your diagram.
4. Look for cross links between causes and effects and draw in lines.
5. By discussion or consensus reaching, agree the main root causes you wish to tackle.

For example:

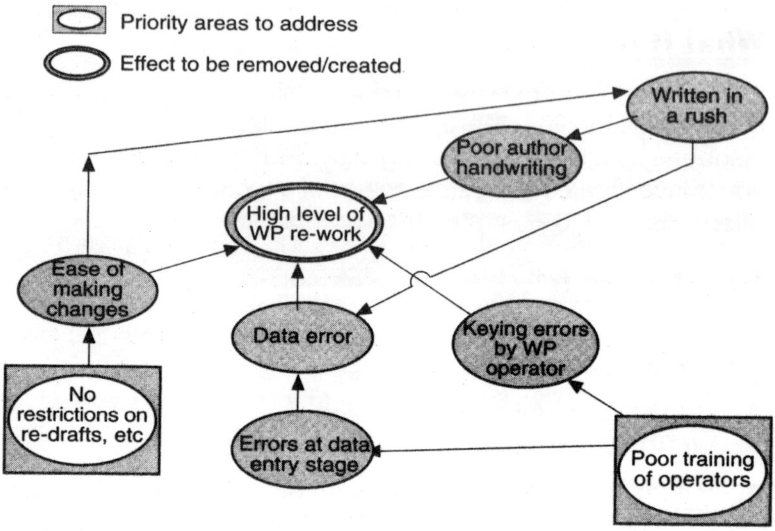

How it helps

Relations Diagrams recognise the fact that there is often not just one simple causal relationship at the root of a problem. They are helpful in illustrating these chains and interconnections and therefore in identifying where to target action. They are also useful for identifying any knock-on effects of these actions.

Swot Analysis

What it is

A SWOT Analysis is a graphical way of summarising a particular process, product, department or organisation in terms of its strengths, weaknesses, opportunities and threats.

How to use it

1. Identify what is to be analysed. Enter this in the centre of your SWOT diagram.

2. Brainstorm the four areas:

Strengths – those internal characteristics/behaviours/ aspects of performance which are strong.

Weaknesses – those internal characteristics/behaviours/ aspects of performance which are weak.

Opportunities – events, openings, changes external to the body being analysed which give positive opportunities for growth or improvement.

Threats – events or changes external to the body being analysed which could be detrimental to pertormance.

List each in the appropriate quadrant of your diagram (see next page).

3. By discussion or voting identify the relative strengths or importance of the factors listed in order to agree priorities for action.

For example:

PRODUCT DEVELOPMENT PROCESS

Strengths

- history of creative and successful product development
- able to start new projects quickly
- accepted use of cross functional teams

Weaknesses

- limited knowledge and experience of latest engineering techniques
- budget restrictions
- limited investment in new technology in recent years

Opportunities

- head of department retires soon
- parent company pushing for new product range

Threats

- competitor Y is rumoured to have re-equipped labs at great expense
- competitor Z is advertising for researchers
- EC likely to impose restrictions on plant testing

How it helps

SWOT Analysis is useful for summarising all the various forces at play in a situation as a starting point for identifying areas for action.

Force Field Analysis can be used as an alternative.

4 Generate ideas and options

Benchmarking

What it is

Benchmarking is the process of learning from others as a basis for setting stretch goals, identifying breakthrough processes and accelerating improvement towards world class performance standards.

How to use it

Benchmarking follows a simple, 7-step process:

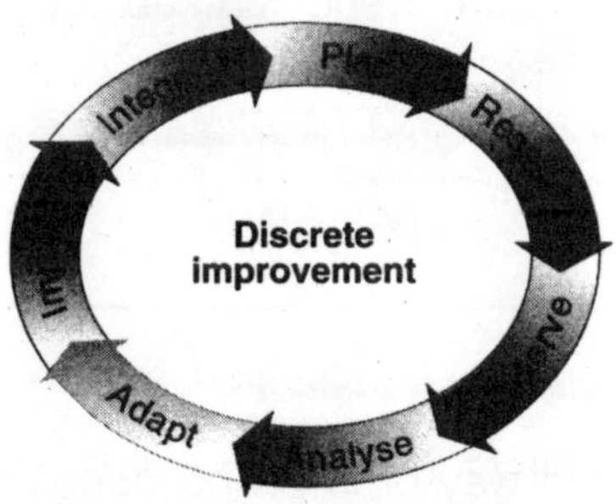

1. **Plan** – decide what to benchmark, when to do it, who to involve and what other resource will be required.
2. **Research** – internally identify existing performance standards and processes.

   Externally identify who to benchmark against and collect as much data as possible from, eg trade press, libraries, contacts and product literature. Don't forget you may be able to benchmark against other companies/divisions in your group.
3. **Observe** – where possible, visit to observe and test the data collected.

4. **Analyse** – dig into the data and observations to identify, eg learning points, new approaches. Compare with your own existing performance. Set breakthrough goals using what you have learnt.
5. **Adapt** – adapt the process, techniques, tools, etc that you have gathered to fit your circumstances and meet your goals.
6. **Improve** – identify ways in which the new process/product can be further improved or enhanced so that you exceed, rather than equal the benchmark.
7. **Integrate** – implement the new process/product rigorously and ensure alignment with other processes and activities. Amend schedules/jobs/layouts, etc to ensure the new way is fully integrated into the business.

Examples of benchmarking:

- An insurance company benchmarked an electricity utility in order to improve their direct debit process.
- A radio pager company benchmarked a pizza parlour to improve local deliveries.
- A manufacturer benchmarked Formula 1 pit teams to improve tool changeover times.

How it helps

Benchmarking is used to systematically:

- identify stretch goals for being world class
- identify ways of achieving improved performance
- help an organisation to learn from others.

Brainstorming

What it is

Brainstorming is a technique which encourages creative thinking and the generation of ideas. Analysis and evaluation are prevented in the early stages of brainstorming ensuring radical and different ideas are aired.

How to use it

1. Assemble the brainstorming group.
2. Appoint a scribe and, if appropriate, a separate timekeeper.
3. Explain the purpose of the meeting and the groundrules. Agree a statement of the topic or issue to be brainstormed. Write this up at the top of the chart.
4. Allocate time to brainstorm and time to review the outputs; 5-20 minutes is usually sufficient for generating ideas, but brainstorms can go on for hours.
5. Agree the groundrules.

   For example:

Groundrules for brainstorming	
No criticism	Crucial if barriers to creative thinking are to be overcome
Encourage wild ideas	All ideas are acceptable
Strive for creativity	Generate as many ideas and volume as possible
Hitch-hike	Build on, add to and combine ideas
List all ideas	No editing or interpretation by the scribe
Incubate	Taking time to reflect on ideas listed often stimulates new thoughts

6. Start the ideas coming – make sure that all ideas are visible to everyone in the group.

   Either allow random contributions or go around the team repeatedly to ensure everyone is involved. Individuals can 'pass' if they have nothing to add.

For example:

Uses of a baked bean tin	
Plant pot	Cooking pot
Pencil holder	Mouses bed
Half a telephone	Measuring tool
Storage	Roller
Leg for broken table	Drinking cup
Rubbish disposal	Bracelet
etc, etc, etc	

7. The scribe should not abbreviate or interpret. It is important to capture ideas exactly as expressed.

SOMETIMES MORE CREATIVE IDEAS ARE PRODUCED BY WORKING IN PICTURES OR ANALOGIES RATHER THAN PLAIN WORDS

8. Having generated a number of ideas, you can then evaluate their usefulness towards meeting the original objective. At this stage, analytical thought and techniques should be used (such as Cause and Effect Analysis, Paired Comparisons, Consensus Reaching).

Before doing this, you may need to seek clarification as not all suggestions may be clear to everyone. Also check for duplications and amalgamate or group similar ideas if appropriate.

How it helps

Brainstorming provides a disciplined (but fun) way to involve people in generating new ideas, so challenging previous assumptions and paradigms.

Force Field Analysis

What it is

Force Field Analysis is a means of identifying the forces that will help or hinder change.

A plan is then developed to harness the positive driving forces and remove, reduce or avoid the negative or resisting forces. Doing so will increase the likelihood of success.

Force Field Analysis can be used in conjunction with Consensus Reaching and Action Plans.

How to use it

1. Define your current situation

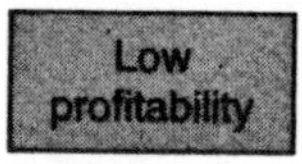

2. Define your target

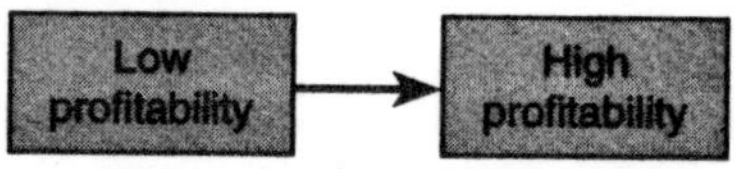

3. Brainstorm the forces which will drive you

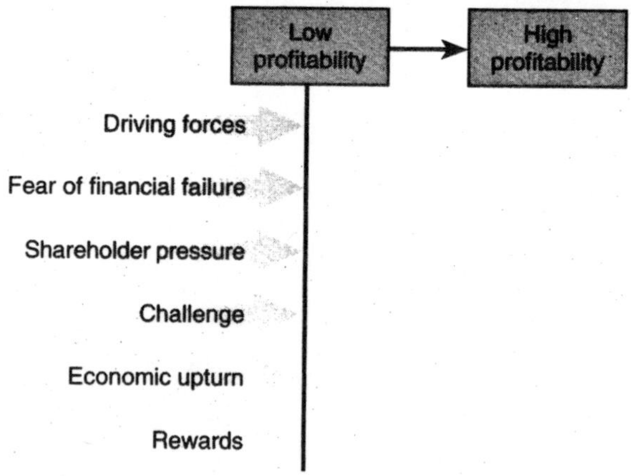

4. **Brainstorm the forces which will restrain you** from achieving your target situation. It is helpful to cover the driving forces when you brainstorm the resisting forces. This will discourage you from simply listing opposites.

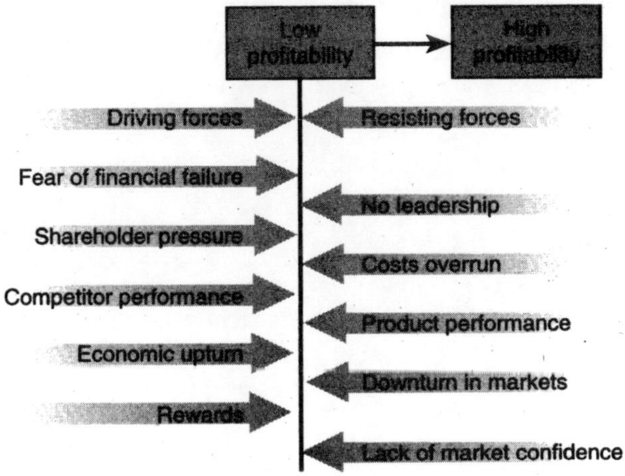

A more sophisticated approach to identifying forces is to use a scale (strong-weak) on each side and draw the arrows in proportion to their strength. This avoids the trap of seeing all forces as equal.

5. **Analyse the forces.** Decide which will have the greatest impact. It is helpful to focus on reducing the resisting forces as this will allow the existing drivers to take you forward more quickly. Consensus Reaching or Paired Comparisons can be used to home in on the most significant force or the one which can be tackled most easily.

6. **Develop an Action Plan** to tackle the main forces which you have identified.

How it helps

Reducing the resisting forces can be more effective than increasing the driving forces. Force Field Analysis is a simple but quick and structured way of reviewing the forces which will help or hinder your success, in order to identify priorities for action. It can be very powerful at turning a negative situation into a more positive one.

Use Mind Mapping

What it is

A mind map is a way of generating and collating ideas and information that is:

- quick to do and use
- non–linear
- pictorial as well as verbal
- more interesting and colourful than text alone
- focused on relationships between ideas.

Mind maps can therefore increase creativity and energy by attracting and involving individuals who think visually and by providing a quick and enjoyable method of generating and assimilating ideas which can increase the enthusiasm of those involved.

How to use it

1. Identify the topic to be covered.
2. Write this in the middle of a large board or piece of paper.
3. Brainstorm the main elements or attributes of the topic. Add each to the mind map as a main branch.
4. For each branch, brainstorm its component parts and add these to the appropriate branch.
5. Whenever possible use pictures, symbols or charts instead of words.
6. Use different colours for different branches so they can be clearly differentiated.
7. If appropriate draw in links between branches and twigs.
8. Review your mind map for completeness and clarity
9. Once completed your map can be used to:

- store information/ideas for future reference
- communicate the output to others
- spark debate about issues and relationships between elements
- develop linear action plans, ie order of priorities, time scales, etc.

For example:

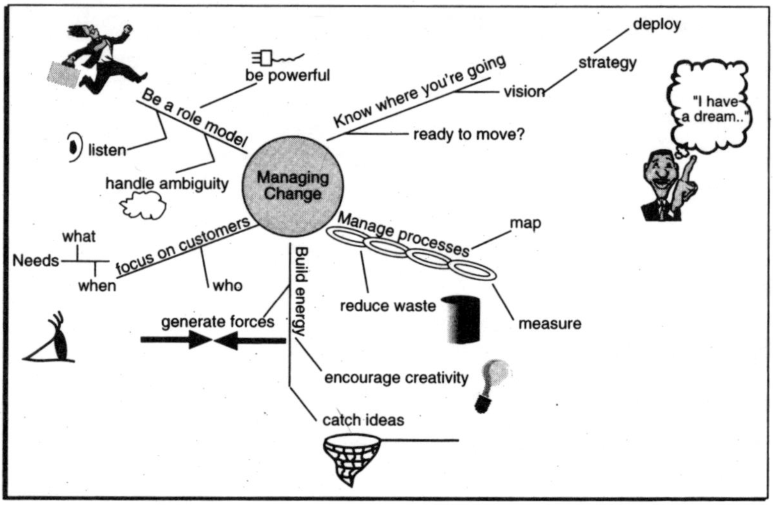

How it helps

Mind-mapping is a fun way of involving people in generating ideas, capturing thoughts and demonstrating the relationships and connections between them; it appeals to visual thinkers as well as those more comfortable with words and avoids the trap of getting into linear thought processes too early.

Six Thinking Hats (De Bono)

What it is

The Six Hats is a general thinking framework which replaces the adversarial thinking of argument and the drift of discussion with constructive parallel thinking. At any moment everyone is thinking in the same direction.

The hats may be used systematically in a sequence but can also be used singly as a symbolic way of requesting a particular type of thinking.

The hats have been shown to reduce meeting times to one quarter of their usual length and to increase productivity up to five fold.

The hats are:

White: (paper) Focus on information. What is available. What is needed. How to get it. Both hard information and soft information.

Red: (fire) Permission to express intuition, feeling and emotion without any need to explain or justify the expression.

Black: (judges' robes) Caution. Risk assessment. Potential problems. Downside. Critical and looking at why something does not fit budget, policy, ethics etc.

Yellow: (sunshine) Focus on benefits and values and ways to make something work.

Green: (vegetation) Everyone seeks to be creative: new ideas, alternatives, possibilities, variations on an idea.

Blue: (sky and overview) Control and management of the thinking process. Defining the problem. Summary, outcome and decision.

How it's done

1. Proper training is recommended.
2. The sequence of hats is determined under the initial blue hat.
3. Everyone wears the same hat at the same time.
4. Decisions, outcomes and next steps are determined under the final blue hat.

How it helps

Speeds up thinking very considerably. Framework for constructive and design thinking. Uses full intelligence and experience of all those taking part. Evaluation is an integral part of the process and decisions usually make themselves by the end of the session. The hats mimic the change in the brain chemistry for different modes of thinking.

(for full information contact:
APTT (USA) 515 278 5570 or, http://www.edwdebono.com/)

5 Make decisions

Consensus Reaching

What it is

Consensus Reaching enables a group of people to arrive at an agreed decision in a structured, time efficient way.

Consensus Reaching involves individual voting against agreed criteria but it is much more than just this as consensus requires unanimous acceptance and support for the chosen solution.

How to use it

1. **Explain the need for a decision**

   Review the circumstances leading to the need to make a decision. Ensure that everyone understands the need.

2. **Brainstorm ideas/alternatives**

   Using Brainstorming groundrules, log ideas/solutions/alternatives.

3. **Check on understanding**

   Ensure that all contributions are fully understood by all present.

4. **Agree decision making criteria**

   Agree the criteria you will use for casting your votes, eg improved service, lowest cost, employee development, personal satisfaction.

5. Determine the number of votes

Give a reasonable number of votes to each member of the group (for example – 10 ideas, two or three votes). Agree the maximum number of votes a member can give to any one idea. One way of deciding this is to count the number of options and multiply this by 0.2 to give the number of votes. (This ensures that voting follows the Pareto principle).

6. Allocate votes

Ask each member to allocate votes to their preferred solution(s) either by shouting them out or coming up to the board and marking them up. Identify the solution(s) with the most votes. If necessary, repeat the process, allocating votes only to the selected solution(s).

As an alternative to voting, where there is only a small number of options, participants can be asked to rank the options in order of preference or priority, ('1' being lowest). These rankings are then totalled. The highest scoring options are preferred the most. (This is sometimes referred to as Nominal Group Technique.)

7. Check for practicality

Review the results – check that the chosen solution(s) or areas to tackle are feasible and realistic and that others are less appropriate.

HINT! REMEMBER MAJORITY AGREEMENT IS NOT CONSENSUS. EVERYONE HAS TO ACCEPT THE WAY FORWARD

For example:

Possible reasons for high staff turnover (identified in brainstorm)	Consensus reaching result (result of giving 6 participants two votes each)
– wage rates	I
– working conditions	0
– poor promotion prospects	I
– management style	~~IIII~~
– competitive labour market	II
– poor induction	III

8. Ask for consensus

Ask each member to state their agreement to the selected solution(s). If this is not easily forthcoming, it is important to explore the reason why and either review the decision again or allay concerns. Otherwise this degenerates into a ranking process and not consensus reaching.

In the example given, management style and poor induction come out as the most likely reasons for high turnover in the view of participants. These two may well be linked. The next step would be to explore exactly what is meant by 'management style'.

If ranking rather than voting had been used the result would have been:

	Individual ranking						Score	Team ranking
Possible reasons	①	②	③	④	⑤	⑥		
– wage rates	2	6	1	3	1	1	14	4
– working conditions	1	2	2	2	2	3	12	6
– poor promotion prospects	3	1	3	1	3	2	13	5
– management style	5	4	6	6	6	5	32	1
– competitive labour market	4	3	4	5	4	4	24	3
– poor induction	6	5	5	4	5	6	31	2

How it helps

This approach enables each member in the group to:

- contribute actively to the decision
- gain a clear understanding of others' points of view.

With the result that:

- the selected viewpoint will have a high degree of acceptance and commitment from everyone.

Consensus Reaching speeds up decision making by giving structure, but should not be used purely as a voting system without discussion.

Cost Benefit Analysis

What it is

Cost Benefit Analysis is a technique for comparing the costs of taking a particular course of action with the financial benefits achievable from the outcome. It is a method of assessing the viability of the course of action in monetary terms. It does not include all types of costs and benefits for example – in terms of customer satisfaction, employee morale or environmental sensitivity and is therefore best used in conjunction with other decision making tools.

How to use it

1. Decide on the period over which the Cost Benefit Analysis will be performed.
2. Identify all of the factors involved which will incur costs or provide benefits. Brainstorming can be used at this stage.
3. Separate the factors into those that incur cost and those that produce monetary benefit. Be sure to identify hidden costs such as parallel running, maintenance, additional training and so on.
4. Assess each of the factors and estimate a monetary value.
5. Add the total costs and the total benefits.

For example: purchase of a small computer

Costs (£)	Year					Total
	1	2	3	4	5	
– Purchase of equipment	1000	–	–	–	–	1000
– Less trade in	200	–	–	–	–	200
– Net cost of purchase	800	–	–	–	–	800
– Maintenance contract	–	150	150	150	150	600
– Training	400	100	100	100	100	800
– Software	500	–	–	200	–	700
– Total costs	1700	250	250	450	250	2900

Benefits (£)	Year					Total
	1	2	3	4	5	
Staff savings	2000	2700	2700	2700	2700	12800
Reduced consumables	400	800	800	800	800	3600
Total benefits	2400	3500	3500	3500	3500	16400

Analysis

Benefit to cost ratio $= \dfrac{\text{Value of benefits}}{\text{Total costs}} = \dfrac{16400}{2900} = 5.6:1$

Net annual benefit (First Year) = Annual benefit – Annual cost
= 2400 – 1700 = £700

Net annual benefit (Average of all years) $= \dfrac{\text{Total benefits} - \text{Total costs}}{5}$

$= \dfrac{16400 - 2900}{5} = £2700$

How it helps

This technique can be used to compare alternative solutions (in conjunction with evaluating the non-financial benefits) in order to objectively identify the best course of action. Cost Benefit Analysis is also commonly used to evaluate the results of a particular course of action.

Decision Chart

What it is

A Decision Chart helps you to identify the best solution out of a range of options by comparing each option against a series of 'musts', 'shoulds' and 'coulds'.

How to use it

1. Agree a clear statement of the problem to be solved or improvement to be made.
2. Brainstorm all possible solutions to achieve your required result.
3. Identify the criteria which need to be satisfied by the solution. Divide these into 'Musts', 'Shoulds' and 'Coulds'.

   'Musts' are criteria which are essential for the solution to be effective;

   'Shoulds' are criteria which are highly desirable to make the solution effective but not 'do or die';

   'Coulds' are criteria which would be nice to have as part of the solution.
4. Develop a matrix to assess performance of the solutions against your 'musts'.

   For example:

Choosing a new car					
	Possible solutions				
Criteria for selection	Model A	Model B	Model C	Model D	Model E
Musts					
1. Seat four people	✔	✔	✖	✔	✔
2. Be under 2000cc	✔	✖	✔	✔	✔
3. Cost less than £12,000	✔	✖	✔	✔	✔
4. Be from a local dealer	✔	✔	✔	✔	✔

5. Eliminate any solutions which do not meet all of your 'must' criteria.

6. Now you can go on to determine how well each of the remaining solutions would meet your needs and how it compares with the other choices. This is done using a weighted rating sheet which involves allocating a value to each 'should' or 'could' which reflects its importance.

Criteria for selection	Possible solutions				
	Weight factor	Model A	Model D	Model E	Max Score
Shoulds					
1. Seat four people	10	8 / 80	9 / 90	10 / 100	100
2. Be under 2000cc	8	7 / 56	6 / 48	5 / 40	56
3. Cost less than £12,000	6	10 / 60	4 / 24	8 / 48	60
4. Be from a local dealer	7	5 / 35	6 / 42	8 / 56	56
Coulds					
5. Have central locking	3	10 / 30	8 / 24	8 / 27	30
6. Have electric windows	5	4 / 20	7 / 35	5 / 25	35
7. Have metallic paint	2	3 / 6	8 / 16	10 / 20	42
Total		287	279	316	379

6.1 Allocate weight factors.

Give the most important criterion '10'. Allocate points 1-10 against all the other criteria showing their relative importance compared to the highest one.

6.2 For each option, rate how well it meets each criterion, allocating points 1-10. Enter in the top left corner of each divided square.

6.3 Multiply the points allocated by the weight factor and enter the total in the bottom right hand corner of each divided square.

HINT!

BEWARE! THIS CAN LOOK VERY OBJECTIVE BUT IT STILL RELIES ON PERSONAL JUDGEMENT

6.4 For each option total the scores for all criteria.

6.5 For each criterion identify the maximum score allocated to any resolution and transfer it to the maximum score box.

6.6 Total the maximum score.

7. The matrix allows you to identify which option has scored highest against your weighted criteria. Comparison of this highest score with the maximum score shows how closely the specific solution matches the best possible.

8. As a final check, assess your options in terms of any likely adverse consequences.

Option	Adverse consequence	Probability	Seriousness
A	eg price rise likely soon	Medium	High
D	eg delays occuring in delivery times	High	Low
E	eg likely to be discontinued	Low	Low

You should now be in a position to assess the best option, given how well each meets your requirements and the likelihood and seriousness of any adverse consequences.

How it helps

Decision Charts help you to make a systematic evaluation of options against a defined list of criteria in order to reach a logical decision on the best option to adopt.

Beware, however, that this is a subjective tool and relies on personal opinion in spite of the impression of objectivity.

Paired Comparisons

What it is

In many situations, several options or alternatives will be available but there is a need to determine which option or combination of options provides the best result.

Paired Comparisons enables a small range of options to be evaluated by choosing between a series of pairs.

How to use it

1. List the options

List the options and alternatives that are to be evaluated on the left hand column of a grid, eg possible opportunities for improvement or alternative solutions.

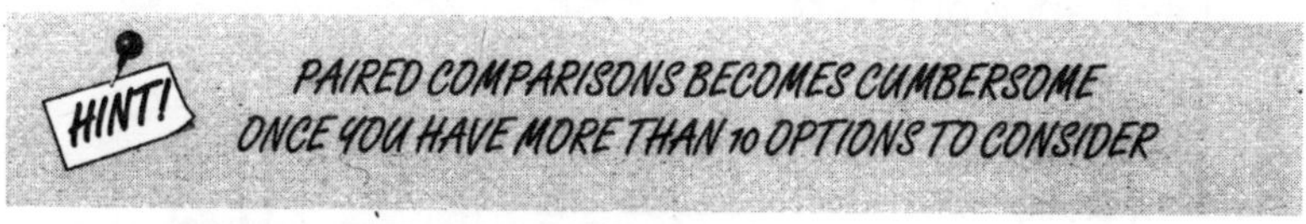

2. Decide evaluation criteria

Determine the question to be used to evaluate the pairs of options, eg which option provides the biggest benefit? Which option is the most likely to be successful? Which option will deliver the quickest results?

3. Compare pairs

Compare option 1 with option 2, determine which is preferred and circle the preferred option on the grid.

Compare option 1 with option 3, determine which is the preferred option and circle the preferred option on the grid.

Continue until option 1 has been evaluated against all the other options.

Then start to compare option 2 with each of the others in turn. Continue until option 2 has been evaluated against all the other options.

This process is continued until all the possible pairs have been evaluated against each other using the evaluation criterion.

4. Count the preferred options

Add up the number of times each option has been chosen and rank in numerical order.

The analysis can be repeated against several different criteria if required and the findings amalgamated.

For example: problem to decide how to spend an inheritance of £2000

No	Options	Paired comparison	Times chosen	Rank
1	Cruise	①/2 ①/3 ①/4 ①/5 ①/6	5	1
2	New bathroom	②/3 ②/4 2/⑤ ②/6	3	3
3	Invest in pension fund	③/4 3/⑤ 3/⑥	1	5
4	Invest in shares	4/⑤ 4/⑥	0	6
5	New wardrobe of clothes	⑤/6	4	2
6	Give it to charity		2	4

Criterion for comparison: Pleasure

How it helps

Paired Comparisons enables priorities to be determined in a quick and qualitative way against agreed criteria.

It is helpful for deciding priorities when numbers of options are available. It can be used either by an individual or by a team.

Priorities Grid

What it is

A Priorities Grid is a tool to help a team decide which option or solution to adopt using the criteria of pay-off and ease of implementation.

How to use it

1. Brainstorm the options available.
2. Assess the pay-off available for each option (if it helps, do a full cost-benefit analysis). Rate each option on a scale from high to low.
3. Assess the ease of implementation of each option in terms of time taken/resources needed/knock-on effects and rate each one on a scale from easy to difficult to do.

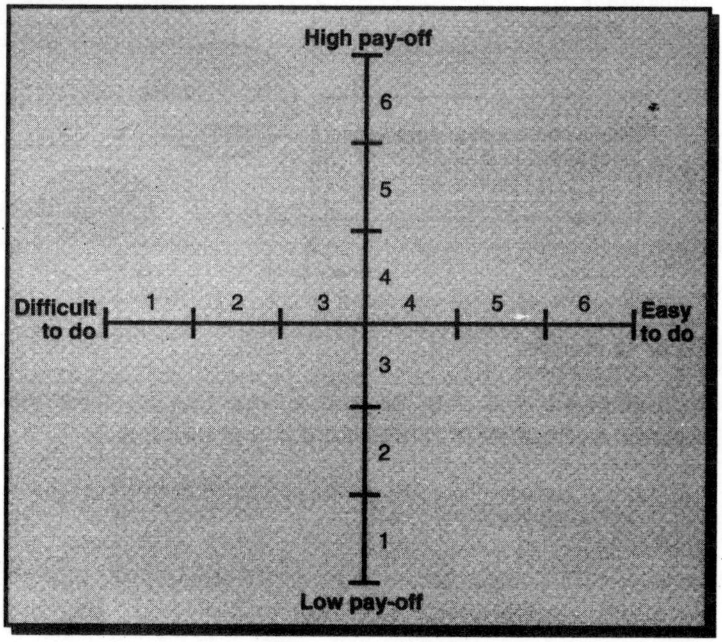

4. Build up a grid to show the relative positions of the options against the two scales. Use Post-it® Notes to do this so that you can easily move the options around on the grid until you are happy they are in the correct relative positions.
5. Clearly, the nearer the top right hand corner of the grid, the better the option. Use the relative positions of all the options to decide which will give the greatest pay-off while being easy to do.

   For example: addressing declining market share

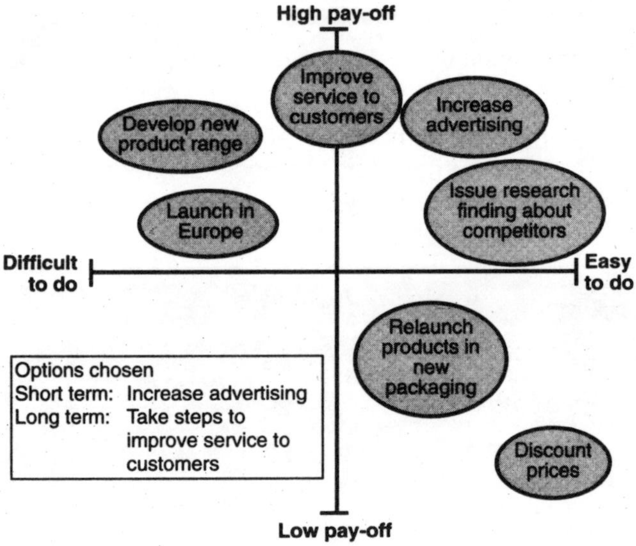

How it helps

A Priorities Grid is a quick and simple tool for differentiating between a range of potential solutions or options.

6 Plan for action

Action Plan

What it is

An Action Plan is an outline of tasks to be undertaken, to achieve a specified objective. It forms the basis of 'getting it right first time'.

How to use it

Action Plans are often shown as charts so they are clear and easy to reference. The typical headings relate to What, Who and When.

Objective		
What needs to be done	Who	When

Action Plans can either be developed in a systematic fashion for a particular project or added to ad hoc for personal use (sometimes referred to as a 'to do' list).

1. Brainstorm all the things which have to be done.
2. Be as specific as possible.
3. Allocate who is going to do it and by when.
4. Look out for discrepancies and resource constraints which will influence the timeframe.

For more complex Action Plans consider using Critical Path or a Gantt Chart.

For example: organising a skiing holiday at the end of February

Objective		
What needs to be done	**By who**	**By when**
Collect brochures from travel agent	Mother	20 Jan
Review brochures to identify options given budget and skiing standards	Children	27 Jan
Agree which holiday to book	All	28 Jan
Book holiday	Father	29 Jan
Check ski-suits still fit	Mother & children	7 Feb
If necessary, replace ski-suits	Mother & children	14 Feb
Organise holiday insurance	Mother	14 Feb
Book airport car parking	Father	21 Feb
Wax skis	All	21 Feb
Cancel newspapers, milk	Mother	24 Feb
Pack	All	27 Feb
Set heating, lights, curtains, etc to maximise house safety while away	Father	28 Feb

How it helps

Preparing an Action Plan helps to:

- identify tasks and priorities
- establish any interrelationships and dependencies
- assign responsibilities
- establish dates by which tasks must be completed.

Critical Path Analysis

What it is

Critical Path Analysis is a way of ordering tasks according to dependencies and time taken. It is therefore useful as a planning technique as well as a monitoring technique, particularly on more complex projects. Critical path charts are also referred to as Arrow Diagrams or Process Decision Programme Charts. They are similar in many ways to Gantt Charts. A Critical Path Analysis shows in a network diagram:

- the critical tasks in terms of impact on total project time
- the most effective way to schedule tasks to achieve the earliest possible target date.

How to use it

1. Brainstorm all the tasks necessary to complete a project (write these on Post-it® Notes, it will save time later).
2. Identify how long each task will take (elapsed time) and record this on the Post-it®.
3. Arrange the Post-its® on a large piece of paper or a board in the order in which tasks can be executed. Start from the left hand side. Look for dependencies and also the possibility of parallel tasking. Remove unnecessary tasks and add any which have been missed.

ALWAYS USE THE SAME UNIT OF TIME FOR EACH TASK

4. Link the Post-it® Notes with lines to show the order in which tasks will be tackled. Use arrows to show the direction of dependencies.
5. Number the Post-it® to show the order in which tasks can be executed.
6. The critical path is the shortest line (in terms of elapsed time) of arrows through the diagram. This shows the minimum time in which the project can be completed.
7. Tasks on the critical path should be started as early as possible, taking into account dependencies and outside constraints.
8. Regularly review progress against the chart and amend as appropriate, particularly if there has been slippage on the critical path.

For example: setting up a training centre (arrow diagram)

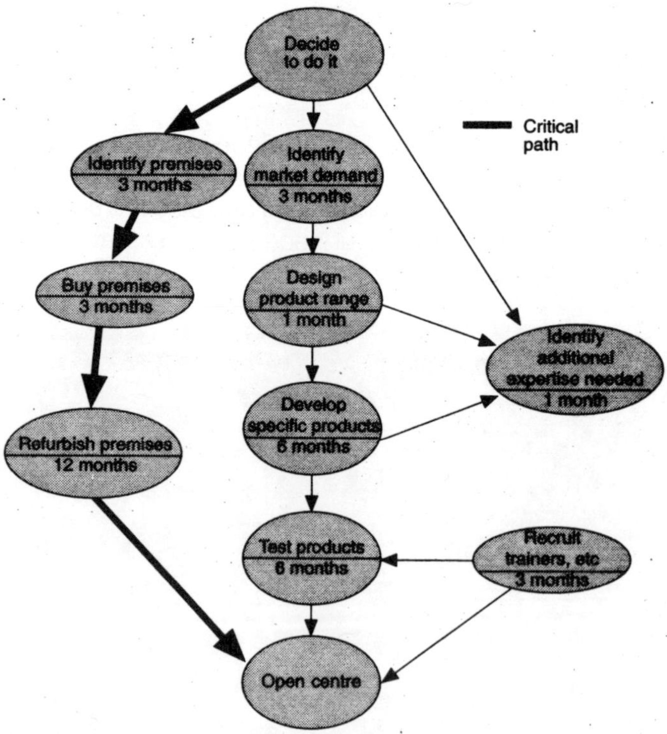

For example: constructing a building (process decision programme chart)

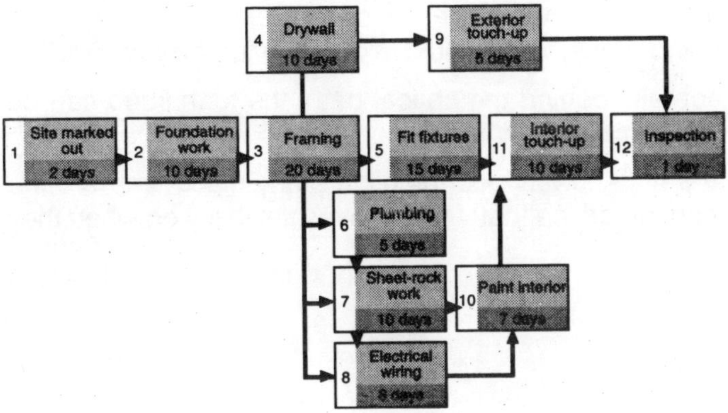

The same data displayed on a Gantt Chart:

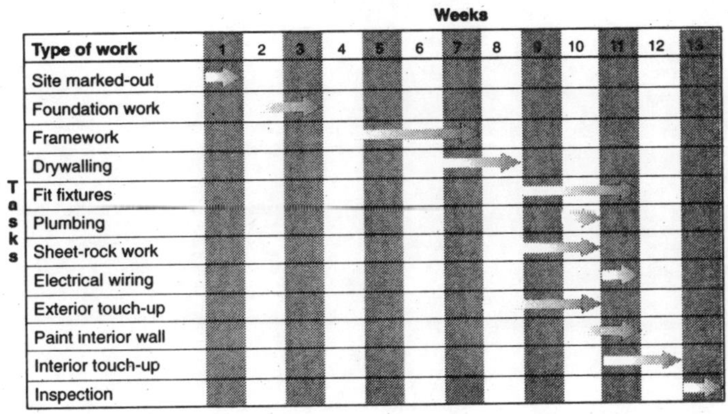

How it helps

Critical Path Analysis is a useful tool for determining the shortest time for achieving a particular task or project and the sequence of events and timing which must take place to achieve this.

If a project falls behind the critical path, the technique can be used to re-estimate the finish time.

A Critical Path Analysis also highlights any slack time around tasks not on the critical path which gives flexibility on when they can be done.

Flag Method

What it is

The Flag Method is a graphical way of combing Pareto Analysis, a Cause and Effect Analysis and Control Charts to illustrate the inputs and progress towards an improvement goal.

How to use it

1. Identify the goal to be addressed.
2. Brainstorm all of the contributory factors which will impact on the goal.
3. Use Pareto Analysis to identify the 'vital few'.
4. Construct a (single-sided) Fishbone diagram linking the vital few to the goal.
5. For each of the main bones identify and add any significant small bones.
6. Add a flag to each level to show percentage target for improvement.
7. Add Control Charts to show progress on the key measures at the goal, main bone and side bone levels.

For example: reducing rejects

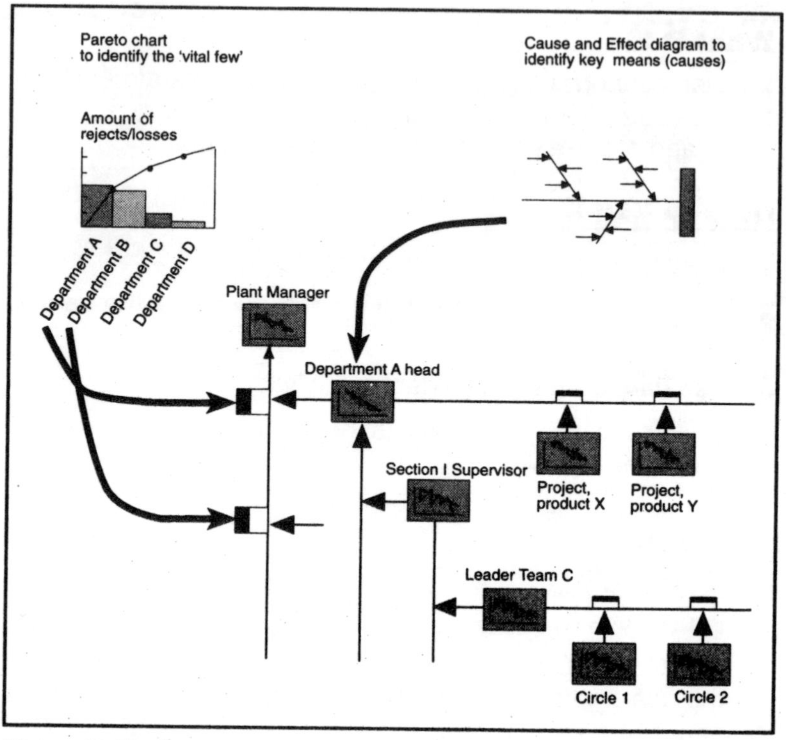

How it helps

The Flag Method is an effective way of planning, communicating and reviewing improvement goals. It is a useful method of displaying/summarising the output from using planning tables.

Gantt Chart

What it is

A Gantt Chart is a simple charting technique to illustrate actions against time, and dependencies between different actions. It is similar to a Critical Path Analysis.

How to use it

1. Brainstorm tasks to be done.
2. Sequence them – look out for dependencies.
3. Size them – in terms of elapsed time.
4. Display on a Gantt Chart spread between start and end times.
5. Check feasibility against overall time available.

Example of a Gantt Chart: project to improve telephone response times

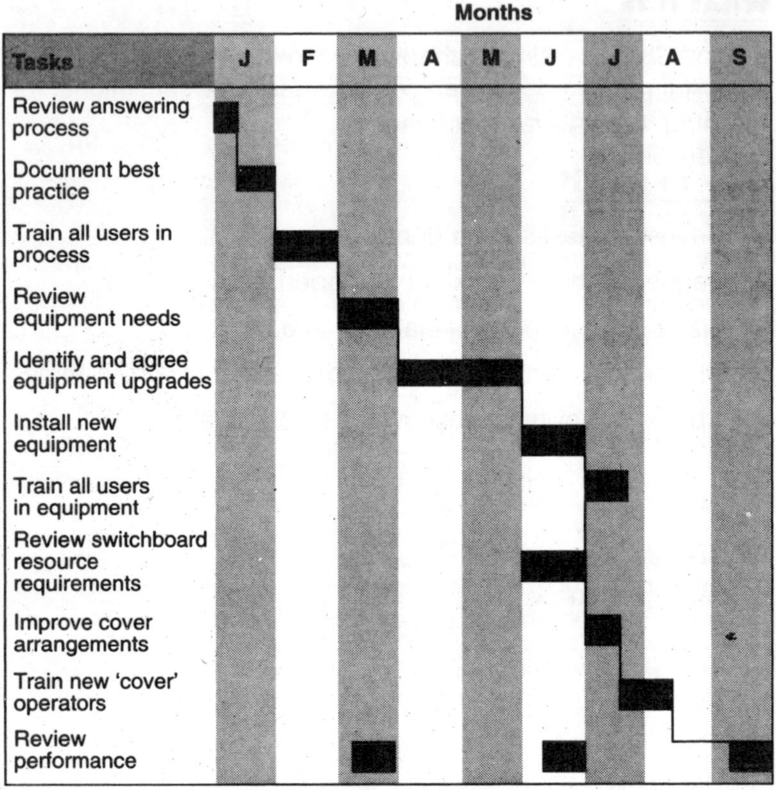

How it helps

A Gantt Chart identifies all the tasks to be done and when they can start and need to finish to complete a project on time. Once complete, the chart can be used for reviewing progress and amending plans as necessary.

Planning Table

What it is

A Planning Table is a simple form for identifying what a particular team/department has to do to contribute to wider objectives. Planning Tables are cascaded through an organisation on a consensus basis.

How to use it

1. Once the overall corporate breakthrough objectives have been identified, directors complete planning tables for the issues or responsibilities assigned to them as owners. If these issues do not fall entirely within their area of functional responsibility, deployment using the planning tables must be agreed with the other relevant directors.
2. The directors must then agree their planning tables with the MD/CEO as a check on realism, alignment, etc.
3. The directors then discuss and agree their improvement strategies with the relevant managers in order to build ownership and develop the next level of detail.
4. This process continues until there is no further scope for developing detailed actions.
5. The planning tables can then be used to regularly review and report progress within the organisation.

For example: cascading planning tables

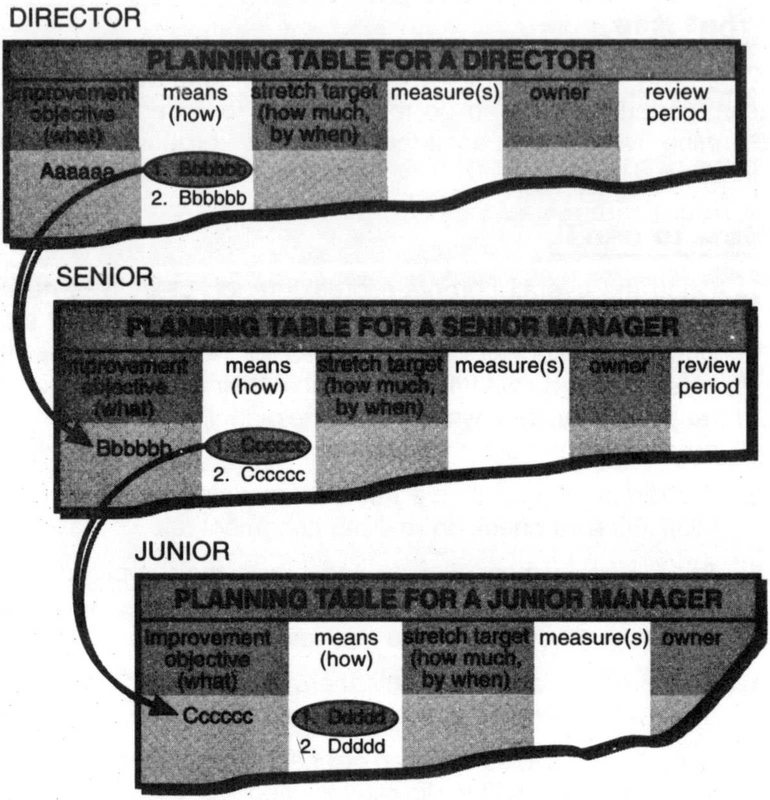

Structured cascade using planning tables

How it helps

A Planning Table gives structure to discussions between individuals/teams and identifies the key areas to be addressed if objectives are to be successfully deployed. Planning Tables are also a clear format for communicating plans and sharing progress.

Tree Diagram
(or systematic diagram method)

What it is

A Tree Diagram is a structured approach to planning that ensures a direct cause and effect relationship between objectives and plans of action. It is most effective when used by a team.

A Tree Diagram is a useful way of summarising a set of planning tables.

How to use it

1. Agree a general statement of the goal or problem to be tackled. Write this in the middle of the left hand side of a large piece of paper (the trunk of the tree). If this statement is already clear enough to action, then it is not necessary to proceed.
2. Identify how this goal can be achieved – brainstorm and prioritise the two to three key means. Write these key means to the right of the goal statement (the branches).
3. Check if these means are clear enough to action. If yes, the process is complete; if no continue. Also check that acting on these means will achieve progress towards the goal. If yes, continue; if no you are probably going off track and you need to go back to step 2.
4. Continue this process of developing more specific means until there is a column of actions at the right hand side of the paper.
5. You are then in a position to go on to complete a matrix diagram or set of planning tables adding in targets, measures and owners.

For example:

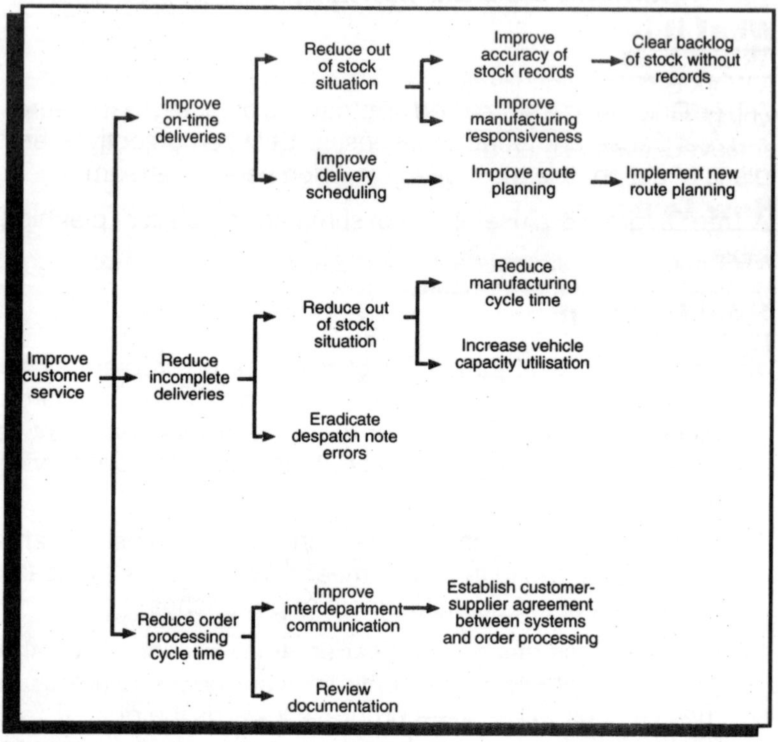

How it helps

A Tree Diagram is a useful tool for breaking down broad objectives into specific actions/projects and ensuring causal links between means and objectives.

It is an effective way of displaying an overview of what is to be done to achieve a particular breakthrough objective.

Work Breakdown Structure

What it is

A Work Breakdown Structure (WBS) is used to identify the tasks which must be completed if an objective or result is to be achieved. (Sometimes referred to as a top down flow chart).

How to use it

WBS involves systematically breaking down an objective until very specific tasks are identified.

1. First define the goal you want to achieve.

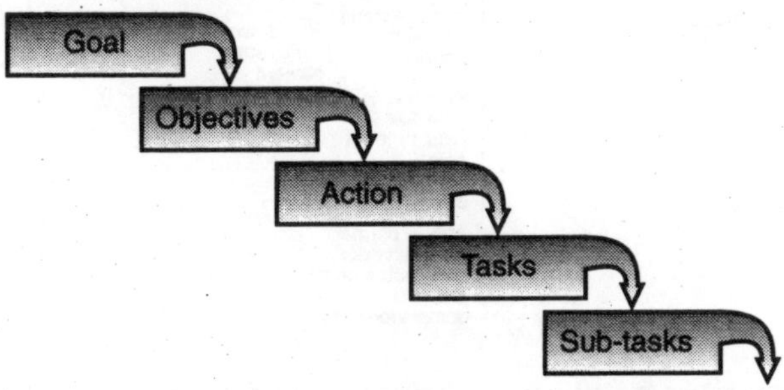

2. Then identify the main means by which the goal is to be met. The required outcomes of each of these can be expressed in the form of enabling objectives or results.
3. List the key actions which must be taken to achieve each enabling objective.
4. For each key action identify the tasks which must be completed.
5. For a task which is sizeable or relatively complex, identify the sub-tasks.
6. Set out the breakdown analysis by using one of the two formats, whichever is most suitable: hierarchy or list. The example shows both formats.

For example: painting the house – hierarchical format

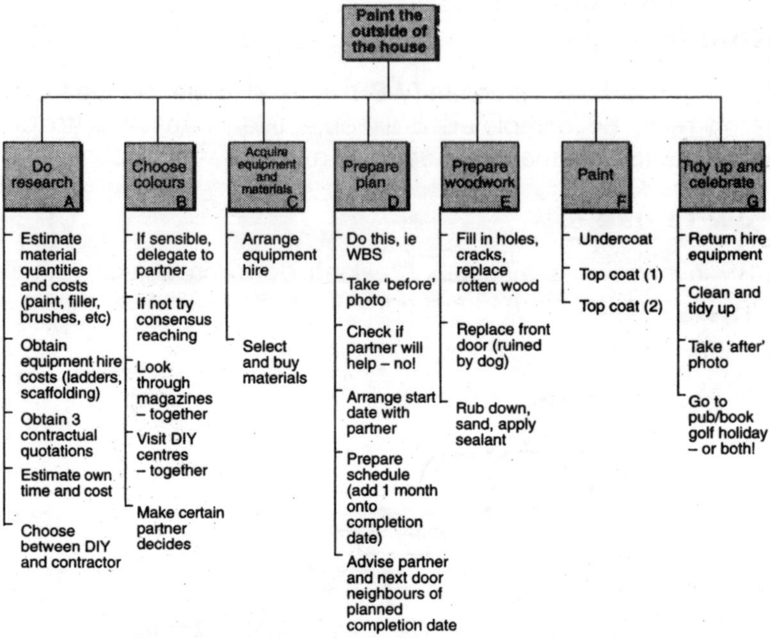

For example: painting the house – list format

A. Do research

1. Estimate material quantities and costs (paint, filler, brushes, etc).
2. Obtain equipment hire costs (ladders, scaffolding).
3. Obtain three contractual quotations.
4. Estimate own time and cost.
5. Choose between DIY and contractor.

B. Choose colours

1. If sensible, delegate to partner.
2. If not, try consensus reaching.
3. Look through magazines – together.
4. Visit DIY centres – together.
5. Make certain partner decides.

C. Obtain equipment and materials

1. Agree equipment hire.
2. Select and buy materials.

D. Prepare implementation plan

1. Do this, ie WBS.
2. Take 'before' photo.
3. Check if partner will help – no!
4. Arrange start date with partner.
5. Prepare schedule (add 1 month onto completion date).
6. Advise partner and next door neighbours of planning completion date.

E. Undertake preliminary preparation

1. Fill in holes, cracks, replace rotten wood, etc.
2. Replace front door (ruined by dog).
3. Rub down, sand, apply sealant.

F. Apply paint

1. Undercoat.
2. Top coat (1).
3. Top coat (2).

G. Tidy up and celebrate

1. Return hire equipment.
2. Clean and tidy up.
3. Take 'after' photo.
4. Go to pub/book golf holiday – or both!

There are certain guidelines for producing a WBS.

1. Only people who know the work should produce a WBS.
2. A WBS can be produced as a whole by a team working together. An alternative approach is to agree the headings: then assign each to one or two people who best know what would be involved and can therefore judge more accurately the level down to which the constituent WBS should be taken.
3. The level of detail to which each arm of a WBS should be analysed will vary according to need.
4. The level of detail to which you should take a WBS should be determined by the level of accuracy and exactness needed, eg to produce a detailed schedule, or roughly estimate resource requirements.

5. A WBS is a preliminary step to producing a schedule and resources estimate. Thus, the timing and ordering of actions or details of responsibilities and man hours involved are not the concern at this stage. The WBS is an aid to defining these requirements simply by listing the main actions or tasks.

How it helps

WBS is a structured way of identifying and presenting the different levels of tasks and activities which must be undertaken to achieve a specific objective or output.

7 The improvement process

Overview of Plan-Do-Check-Act

What it is

Plan-Do-Check-Act is a systematic improvement process for solving Quality problems and implementing lasting solutions.

How to use it

PLAN

1. Select an opportunity for improvement
2. Identify the customer's desired outcome
3. Define the problem
4. Collect data
5. Analyse for root causes
6. Find solutions
7. Prepare plan to implement solution

DO

8. Implement solution

CHECK

9. Monitor results, evaluate against plan
10. Determine reasons for deviation

ACT

11. Take corrective action or deviations
12. Standardise the process – make successful solutions permanent
13. Reflect

PLAN

1. Select an opportunity for improvement

- Generate a list of opportunities for improvement.
- Before selection, make sure all the possible options are identified.
- Prioritise and select an opportunity.

2. Identify the customer's requirements

- Specify the customer by name.
- Know and analyse the customer requirements.
- Be prepared to help the customer to define their requirements precisely.
- Develop a Customer-Supplier Agreement.

3. Define the problem

- How do the customer's requirements compare with the current situation?
- Define the problem to be solved.

4. Collect data

- Define and map the current process.
- Select measurements needed: before, during and after the process.
- Collect data for analysis.
- Prepare Process Map.

5. Analyse for root causes

- Do Cause and Effect Analysis and identify probable causes.
- Select the most probable causes and test if the root cause has been found.
- Define the root cause(s) of the problem.

6. Find solutions

- Develop criteria for solutions.

- Identify 'musts' versus 'wants'.
- Generate possible solutions, evaluate against the 'musts', 'shoulds', etc and select the best available solution.
- Do Cost Benefit Analysis.

7. Prepare plan to implement solution

- Determine the expected improvement. Set specific goals for improvement.
- Prepare initial action plan.
- Identify driving and resisting forces using Force Field Analysis and amend your plan accordingly.
- Finalise and agree the plan.
- Build in check points to monitor progress.
- If necessary, gain approval to implement the solution.

HINT! NOTICE THE NUMBER OF STEPS IN THE PLAN PART OF THE PROCESS COMPARED WITH THE DO, CHECK AND ACT PARTS OF THE QUALITY IMPROVEMENT CYCLE

DO

8. Implement the plan

- Carry out the plan, implement the solution.

CHECK

9. Monitor results – evaluate against plan

- Measure success against the customer's requirements and feedback.
- Is the customer delighted?

- What benefits can be measured?
- Monitor implementation against check points – do not leave until implementation is complete.

10. Determine reasons for deviations

- Where was the plan not successful?
- Ask why?

ACT

11. Correct action for deviations

- Based on an understanding of why parts of the plan were not successful, develop revised plans.

12. Standardise the process – make sure the successful solution is permanent

- Make sure the gains that have been achieved are made permanent. (This involves stabilising the improved process).

13. Reflect

- What have we learned? What have we achieved? What's our start point for further improvement?

REMEMBER IT IS: READY AIM FIRE!
NOT READY FIRE AIM! BUT ALSO BE AWARE OF:
READY AIM AIM AIM... AIM!

How it helps

The improvement process helps solve problems and identify/ implement solutions in a disciplined way. When all managers and staff use the same process, teamwork can be significantly enhanced.